**BY RICHARD M. LANGWORTH
AND THE EDITORS OF CONSUMER GUIDE®**

Great Cars From *Ford*

CASTLE
BOOKS

Louis Weber, President
Publications International, Ltd.
3841 West Oakton Street
Skokie, Illinois 60076

This edition published by:
Castle Books
A Division of Book Sales, Inc.
110 Enterprise Avenue
Secaucus, N.J. 07094

Manufactured in the United States of America
1   2   3   4   5   6   7   8   9   10

Library of Congress Catalog Card Number: 82-80152

ISBN: 0-89009-537-X

Principal Author: Richard M. Langworth

Contributing Author: Jan P. Norbye

Photo Credits: Bill Buffa, Carol George, Ford Motor
Company Photomedia Department; John Apolinski;
David Gooley; Phil Hall; Richard M. Langworth; Shelby
American Automobile Club. Special thanks to John Hruby
and Fred Lorenzen.

Cover Design: Frank E. Peiler

Contents

1912 Model T Runabout

Introduction: A Matter of Perfect Timing

*F*ord Motor Company celebrated its 75th anniversary in 1978. Over the next few years, as the auto industry faced unprecedented financial losses and new challenges on almost every front, some pundits predicted the firm would not see its 100th.

We think that assessment is far too gloomy. Ford's astounding success in the Teens, its prosperity during the 1920s, its rebirth in the late '40s, and its high stature in the '50s and '60s were not, after all, the result

of some magic formula. In fact, the firm's entire history could be fairly described by its one-time slogan, which is still used today: Ford had better ideas.

The cars in this book are the best—and best-loved—examples of why Ford "made it." Every one of them was a "better idea," though some were better than others. What they all shared was a special quality—call it uniqueness if you will—that kept people interested in and enthusiastic about the cars from Dearborn. But besides interest value, what was it that made these cars so successful?

It wasn't quality. Except for the Model A and the prewar V-8s, most of the "Great Cars from Ford" weren't built any better than more recent models. It wasn't sophistication. There was nothing sophisticated about a Model T. Even the complicated Skyliner retractable hardtop of the '50s was more a cantankerous Rube Goldberg device than an engineering *tour de force*. No, what all Ford's best have in common, if we have to pick one word, is *timing*. They all appeared at precisely the right moment, the moment when buyers discovered or felt a need for something new, something better, something distinctive. And because these cars met their needs, people admired them.

Take the Model T, for instance. When it appeared for 1908, America had just realized there were better ways to get around than on or behind a horse. Henry Ford was also able to sell his Tin Lizzy for as little as $260—worth a lot more then than $260 is today, granted, but it wasn't all *that* much more than a good horse and buggy cost. Cheap to buy, cheap to run, quirky but lovable, the Model T literally put the nation on wheels, and made the irascible Henry one of the country's industrial legends.

Go on to the Model A. Again, the timing was perfect. By 1929 the Tin Lizzy was obsolete; there were better cars available for just a little more money. Chevy's success in the late '20s suggested that, but the Model A confirmed it. Of course, this new Ford had to be good, and it was. Today, there are many former Model A owners who wish they'd never parted with theirs, not to mention millions of younger fans who discovered the car generations after the last one left the factory.

Or, take the monobloc V-8, the famed "flathead." Again, Ford's timing couldn't be faulted. When it arrived in 1932, people had begun to crave swifter acceleration and greater refinement to match the more modern styling, more comfortable ride, and more advanced engineering cars were beginning to acquire. But performance just wasn't available in a low-price car. The V-8 changed all that, ushering in an era that would last half a century.

The Fords of significance in the postwar years continued to be marked by astute timing. The wood-bodied 1946–48 Sportsman convertible was conceived to renew interest in a line of cars which, of necessity, were based on a prewar design. The 1950 Crestliner sedan was created to satisfy the public's appetite for pillarless "hardtop convertibles" until Ford's own hardtop was ready. The glass-roof Skyliner did other hardtops one better in 1954. The public's fascination with exotic dream cars and futuristic features made the 1957–59 Skyliner retractable hardtop a sensation, even if it didn't sell well. The Thunderbird came along exactly when people were beginning to appreciate sports cars. Then, Ford shrewdly made it into a four-seater for 1958, and the personal-luxury car was born. The Mustang is probably the best example of adroit timing in the entire history of the American automobile industry.

The Mustang and T-Bird, of course, are the two most singular examples of Ford's market leadership—products that started trends rather than merely mirrored them. Lately, it might seem the firm has lost its sense of timing. Look at Fords of the '70s and '80s and you might be tempted to say Dearborn has been beset by the "inertia syndrome." That's the attitude which says "let's do nothing, because something might go wrong." It's an attitude that would be more likely to occur at Ford than any other auto company. After all, this is the firm that produced stunning successes like the Falcon and Mustang and appalling failures like the Edsel with equal ease.

Has Ford lost its sense of timing? Has it lost the ability to be on the scene with the right cars at the right time? There's evidence—and recent evidence at that—to suggest the answer is no. The smaller, lighter, more economical 1974 Mustang II, for example, arrived right after the Arab oil embargo that touched off the first "energy crisis." In its first model year, Mustang II came within 10 percent of equalling the huge sales success of the original 1965 Mustang. The subcompact Pinto departed in disgrace following a landmark trial over the design of its fuel tank and filler neck. But it should not be forgotten that this simple little car—surely the '70s equivalent of the Model A—lasted for 10 model years and sold in far greater numbers than Chevy's technically more advanced, but far less reliable, Vega. And the Pinto's replacement was the front-wheel-drive Escort, a modern world-class car which has been developed into a true import-fighter in an amazingly short time.

There are other examples. The current Ford Mustang (and its Mercury Capri twin) provides an alternative to sporty import coupes, and is far and away the best-seller in its field. The compact Fairmont may be dull, but in size and concept it's the closest thing to a Mercedes or Volvo you can buy with a "Made in America" stamp. More importantly, it has been highly successful. The two-seat Ford EXP/Mercury LN7 is an interesting idea, and promises to become even more so in the next few years. Indeed, it may be the start of another trend—the practical personal car.

A final word. Ford's success, like that of Chevrolet, has never depended on interesting or unique products, though they have certainly played a part in it. It is, rather, the bread-and-butter models sold in great numbers that have kept the company in business. That's just as true in the '80s as it was in the heyday of the Model T or the Model A. So, perhaps the real "Great Cars from Ford" are the ones owned and driven by millions of people—the ones each of us remember with special affection simply because they provided dependable daily transportation and thus became such a familiar and important part of our lives. There may even be one in your driveway right now—a scruffy Fairmont, a brand new LTD, or any of a hundred others we could name.

And if, after reading this book, you feel the urge to go out and give your Ford a more thorough than usual wash and polish job, go ahead. We understand.

The 1921 Model T Runabout

Model T: Motoring for Millions

More than seven decades after its introduction, the Model T Ford seems little more than a quaint curiosity. Because of that, it is easy to lose sight of its importance. The Model T is the spiritual ancestor of virtually every car on the road today.

Unlike the hundreds of horseless carriages built before it, the Model T was not a handcrafted, one-of-a-kind "motorcar." Nor was it a rich man's toy priced hundreds or even thousands of dollars above what the common man could afford. Nor was it Henry Ford's first car. Its letter designation indicates there were earlier Ford models, which represented considerable time, effort, thought, and experience. They were the necessary first steps that made the Model T what it was.

And what it was certainly was a revolution. For a generation it was the main means of travel for millions of Americans who both loved and hated it. Despite several infuriating characteristics, it was a definite step forward from the horse and buggy. More significantly, it was reliable, durable, and adaptable to all sorts of transportation needs. Simply put, the Model T changed American lives and America's landscape by proving the automobile was an idea that worked.

When Henry Ford died in 1947, obituaries hailed him as "the father of the automobile." In fact, he was not, although anyone who had owned or known a Model T—and that meant just about everybody—would not think to question the epitaph. But with the beloved Tin Lizzy, Henry could be said to be the father of the automobile industry as we know it today. The Model T was the first car built by the thousands, not one at a time, on a production line employing sequential assembly. And it was one of the earliest to embody the principle of interchangeable parts. Both these factors, not to mention its simple design, allowed the Model T to be sold at very low prices well within the reach of a vast number of people who had never been able to afford a car before. And that, of course, is the main reason why the Model T became so universal—and so significant.

Small-scale assembly line methods and standardized parts were in use before the Model T, both at Ford and elsewhere. The idea of a moving production line was probably conceived by Ransom Eli Olds, whose cars were once the number-one sellers in the country. But it was Henry Ford who perfected the idea. His Model N and Model S, toward the end of their production runs, were built by means of a "sequential floor plan," in which machines and manpower were strategically located to "add" to each car as it proceeded on its orderly way through the factory.

It was with the Tin Lizzy, however, that the large-volume assembly line we know today was introduced to the automobile industry. Even then, the idea wasn't applied to the early Model Ts—it had to wait until 1913. It was in that year that Ford foreman William C. Klann had his "better idea." According to Henry, Klann's notion of having the cars move slowly past worker stations (towed along by a rope at first, later by an endless chain) stemmed "from the overhead trolley that the Chicago meat packers used in dressing beef." Whatever its origins, it was a stroke of genius.

The production line cut Ford's assembly time in half—then quickly halved it again. From 78,440 cars in 1912, Ford output zoomed to 168,220 in 1913, then shot to half a million just three years later. Through mass production, the Dearborn factories built more than 15 million Model Ts between 1907 and 1927. It was a single-model record that would stand until the 1960s, when it was surpassed by another car of universal popularity, the Volkswagen Beetle.

Because it may be unfamiliar to those too young to remember it first hand, let's briefly describe the car that once was as common as goggles and duster coats on the rugged, rutted roads of early 20th Century America. The Model T used a side-valve, three-main-bearing, four-cylinder engine with the cylinders cast *en bloc*. Displacement was 176.7 cubic inches, and compression ratio was 4.5:1. "It will run," as one contemporary wag put it, "on almost anything from gasoline to a good grade of kerosene." That's maybe a shade optimistic, but octane level certainly didn't matter to a Tin Lizzy. Lubrication was accomplished with a combination of gravity and splash systems. Cooling was by means of the thermosyphon system in the later years when the vast majority of Ts were produced. The sturdy 100-inch-wheelbase chassis featured a beam axle and transverse leaf spring at the front—and the very same arrangement at the rear. Mr. Ford saw no need for a different suspension layout or geometry at each end of his "Universal Car."

The key to making the thing move was Ford's patented planetary transmission, built in unit with the engine. The tail end of the transmission housing had a ball and socket joint that received the ball front of the driveshaft and took the driving thrust (along with radius rods) from the rear wheel bearings. On cars built after 1908 (about 95 percent of all Model Ts), the transmission was controlled with what one writer termed "the three most famous pedals in the world." These were marked "C," "R," and "B"—presumably to prevent novice drivers from forgetting. Pedal "C" (clutch) worked a band, located inside the transmission, that engaged one of the two forward speeds. Pedal "R" (reverse) was connected to a similar reverse band, and was used for the obvious purpose. Pedal "B" (brake) operated a brake band that simply stopped the driveshaft from rotating, which brought the car to a halt. The gas tank was housed under the front seat, and getting fuel to the engine was strictly a matter of gravity.

The Model T's three famous pedals

After checking fuel level (by peering into the tank), the driver fired up with a few healthy cranks on the starter handle. (An electric starter became an option in 1919.) Once the engine was chugging, it was time to adjust the spark by means of a lever on the left side of the steering column. Dyed-in-the-wool T-drivers took pride in knowing precisely where to set the spark and throttle levers before starting and how to adjust the choke just so. "We all had to know the hand-cranking procedure, with the choke wire by the radiator," remembers longtime T-driver Robert Bateman. "Your left toes knew the pressure and angle to hold it in neutral while you released the handbrake-cum-clutch-neutralizer. The idea was to shove in the pedal to get to low speed as fast as possible, because a slow application wore out the bands. When you judged the speed sufficient for the load and grade you eased back into high, controlling the gas lever at the same time."

Bateman makes it sound easy. The complete Model T shifting drill is extremely complicated for the first-time driver. A newcomer, who may not appreciate that Lizzy isn't just another car, will invariably push the right pedal to accelerate and the left to declutch—with predictable results. It usually took at least a year of practice, John Keats once wrote, before the Model T pilot "could get into high without bounding down the road looking like a frog with St. Vitus' dance and sounding like a canning factory with something wrong with it."

Braking in a Model T is also an interesting exercise, which new drivers attempt only because . . . well, a T is so unbreakable (no pun intended). If it does hit anything, chances are it will just bounce off. To stop, you would ostensibly stomp on the "B" pedal, but this rarely does more than slow the pace a little. The aforementioned lefthand brake/declutch lever is usually needed, and it doesn't hurt to jab the "R" pedal on occasion, either.

The seating position in any Tin Lizzy is towering. The commanding view allows you to look *down* on the car's hood from a perch that is level with the roofs of most cars built after 1955 or so. Roadholding, given the rudimentary suspension, is quite good. A Model T really isn't fast enough (only 35–40 mph tops) to put it to a severe test, which it would undoubtedly fail in a hurry. Steering, with four turns lock-to-lock, is fairly fast even by modern standards. The only steering reduc-

1910–11 Model T Touring Car

1915 Model T Center Door Sedan

1913 Model T Town Car

1916 Model T Touring Car

Henry Ford (right) and friends with Model T "Fore Door" Touring, circa 1912

Early-'20s Model TT Panel Delivery

tion is a planetary gearset under the steering wheel. The lower end of the steering shaft has a bolt-on lever which pushes or pulls a rod working on the tie rod, located between the spindle arms.

Hills present a special challenge. Usually the Model T driver would approach one either flat out (by getting a running start) or—to make it to the top of steeper grades—in reverse. There were two reasons for this. First, reverse was geared higher (4:1) than low (3:1). Second, the gravity-feed gas tank was placed higher than the carburetor. Unless the tank was full, the car would stall going forward up a grade of one-in-five or steeper. And there was a reason for that. The gravity/splash lube system was not fully effective at such angles. Ford had placed the gas tank so as to eliminate the chance of oil starvation on steep grades!

Henry Ford saw no need to change the Tin Lizzy through 1915, the year in which the millionth Ford was produced. Brass trim was removed—the headlights

and horn in 1916 and the radiator shell (which was painted black, naturally) the following year. Henry did nothing for another seven years, then introduced his "modernized" Model T, which really wasn't too different from the 1922 version. One important step, however, was the addition of a new four-door model (called Fordor, of course), which gave Lizzy a short extra lease on life. Sales were enormous in 1923–24 as Ford made an average $50 per car and netted $100 million total profit.

Meanwhile, the competition was preparing to put an end to the Model T's incredible market domination. General Motors, reorganized after the 1920 recession by Pierre duPont and Alfred Sloan, was readying a Chevrolet only slightly more costly than the Ford and yet far more modern and better-looking. Although Henry cut prices in 1924—down to an unheard of $265 for the runabout—the opposition slowly gained sales ground. Calendar year production figures are illuminating:

Lizzy's rugged chassis, 1924

1919 Model T "High Body" Coupe

1924 Model T Touring Car with side curtains

1925 TT Side Screen Delivery Truck

1923 Model T Touring Car

1926 Model T Sports Touring

Year	Ford	Chevrolet
1924	1,749,827	262,100
1925	1,643,295	444,671
1926	1,368,383	588,962

For a time, Mr. Ford refused to see the writing on the wall. For 1925 he offered an optional nickel-plated radiator and balloon tires to improve Lizzy's looks, and again dropped prices to record lows—as little as $260 for the roadster. For 1926 he made the nickel radiator shell standard, and offered a choice of colors for the first time since 1913—blue, gray, brown, and the perennial black. But it would not be enough. Chevrolet, Dodge, Buick, and Hudson (the latter through its popular Essex) produced about as many cars between them as Ford. In 1926, Ford's volume was still substantial, but by then even Henry realized it couldn't last forever.

Ford carried on with a 1927 version of the T, standardizing wire wheels and adding green and maroon to the color choices. In late May of that year, the last T rolled out of Dearborn. Henry closed the factory doors to tool up for an all-new model. Against a 1927 volume of only 356,000 Fords, Chevrolet won the production race with 1.75 million units. It was the first time since 1905 that Ford had not been America's number-one seller.

A wealth of genius followed in Henry Ford's footsteps, contributing greatly to the evolution from his Universal Car to the automobiles we know today. But if you really want to know what motoring was all about in the days when motorists were usually thought of as rakehell adventurers, you might want to look up the owner of a Model T Ford. If it's one of those mild autumn days just before the frost gathers, when orange and crimson leaves dapple in the sunlight over still-surviving dirt roads, don't be surprised if no one's home. He's probably just gone for a drive.

1931 Model A Convertible Sedan

Model A:
The Interim Miracle

*H*enry Ford made the decision to replace the Model T in July 1926. That same year, Ford Motor Company began suppressing sales figures—and no wonder. In 1924, Ford had sold 600,000 more cars than all the other manufacturers combined; in 1925 sales were 350,000 less. During 1926, the competition sold two cars to every Ford.

Henry had hoped to hang on with the Model T until he could perfect his radical X-car. Typically, this would have been a unique machine. Its engine was an eight with a double-X configuration, four pairs of cylinders on a single crankshaft. Though Ford continued to toy with the X-8 after the Model A appeared, the idea never proved workable.

But the X-8 did lead to the Model A simply because of that. An unsigned memorandum found in the Ford Archives and dated January 16, 1926 outlined the scenario. The Model T needed to be replaced immediately; the X-8 wasn't ready; therefore, Ford needed a stopgap car, which the memo suggested be a six. Henry bought the proposal but not the six-cylinder engine, which he despised. Sixes, he said, had all the problems of eights and none of their advantages. So, he decided to stick with a four. More importantly, though, he finally agreed to replace the Model T. As we now know, the Model A was an interim car, as the

memo suggested. In just four years it would be replaced by the Ford V-8. But it was also a miracle of engineering, created in less than 18 months.

The Model A engine project officially began on August 7, 1926 when young Larry Sheldrick, an engineer from Lincoln Division who had been involved in the X-8 project, was "commissioned to start the designs of a new 4-cylinder engine of larger displacement for a new car to replace the Model T." Sheldrick's reminiscences, on file in the Ford Archives, indicate that it was decided early on to give the engine a bore and stroke of 3⅞ by 4¼ inches for 200.5 cubic inches, about 12 percent more displacement than the Model T.

Contrary to several accounts, the Model A project was not started after the last Model T was built, but long before. However, the period between May 1927, when the last T was built, and December, when the first A was sold, had a profound effect on the company. Henry Ford counted the money he had in the bank before and after the Model A project was completed, and said the whole thing had cost him $100 million. In fact, it was closer to $250 million. It included not only the costs for the required new tooling and shifting production to the great Rouge plant, but also the costs of not having a car to sell for seven months. What it didn't account for were the many dealerships Ford lost in that crucial interim through both defections and bankruptcy.

Mr. Ford wasn't moved by any of this. All his life he remained convinced that people would accept any and all hardship in exchange for the privileges of receiving whatever it was he was planning for them. What saved him was that what he had in mind was invariably good.

Henry would settle for nothing less than 40 bhp from the new four-cylinder engine—double the T's output—despite the small gain in displacement. It was a tall order, and Sheldrick's first prototype was measured on the dynamometer at no more than 22. In a heated discussion, Edsel Ford told the Engineering staff that if they didn't have the talent to develop a 40-bhp engine in-house, he'd go elsewhere. The production boss, "Cast Iron" Charlie Sorensen, saved the day. An engineer named Harold Hicks in the aircraft division had had experience with high-power engines, Sorensen said, and suggested bringing him over. According to company records, Hicks took just three weeks (he was given four) to obtain the required 40 bhp and a 55–60-mph cruising speed. He redesigned the manifold to improve breathing, widened the exhaust valve water passages, and replaced the Holley carburetor with a Zenith.

Henry Ford looked at what Hicks had done and accepted it all—except for that Zenith carburetor. Hicks had been afraid of this; Henry was a close friend of George Holley. But it was the number of bolts in the Zenith carburetor that bothered Mr. Ford. It had too many. Zenith was told to redesign and reduce it to two. Still too many, said Henry. Accordingly, the production Model A carburetor had just a single bolt.

Otherwise, Henry was delighted with Hicks' work, and told the engineer to take out a prototype car and "pass everything in sight." Hicks did just that until he encountered a driver who wouldn't stay passed. The other car swerved to the left and demolished the Ford. Hicks survived with a few cuts and a battered arm after being thrown to the windshield. That was enough for Henry and Edsel. The new car would have safety glass all around. It was to be another first in the low-priced field.

Henry was less happy when Edsel informed him that the T's planetary transmission would also have to be replaced, and for a time he balked. Sliding-gear transmissions didn't stand up, he said (though somehow he had no trouble with them in Lincolns). What about an automatic planetary? That would take years, Edsel and Sorensen told him, and they just didn't have the time. Ultimately, Henry gave in, and engineer Frank Johnson devised a sliding-gear transmission based on the Lincoln unit, though smaller, of course.

Henry contributed as much to the project as he criticized, though. After a personal test ride (he made those often: "Somebody," he said, "must represent the public") he decided the Model A's ride was too hard. So, he specified hydraulic shock absorbers, an unheard-of luxury for a car in this class. The Model A got them. (And, in due course, so did the competition.)

A U-section ladder chassis with three crossmem-

1928 Model A Standard Sport Roadster

1928 Model A Standard Sport Roadster

1929 Model A Standard Phaeton

1930 Model A Roadster Pickup

bers and transverse leaf springs front and rear was the only way in which the Model A resembled the Model T, but even here there were differences. The A made more use of stamped, instead of forged, steel for suspension pieces. Henry had at first insisted that all components be forged; he didn't trust pressed steel.

Model A Station Wagon, new for '29

1929 Model A Fordor Sedan (body by Briggs)

1929 Model A Standard Roadster

1930 Model A Tudor Sedan interior

Sorensen finally changed his mind by a demonstration in which he alternately sat on forged and pressed steel pieces of the same configuration. Neither one bent. Using pressed steel was what today would be termed "cost-effective." But Henry was his own cost analyst in 1926, and was quite willing to say "hang the cost," as he did with the safety glass.

There was nothing in the Model A's development that involved the sort of laborious testing and redesign that go into an all-new car today. None of Henry's engineers were graduates of higher institutions. They all worked by the "seat-of-the-pants" method, and they all ultimately reported to Henry Ford—in person. Testing, such as it was, was rudimentary. Test driver Ray Dahlinger invariably had only two possible evaluations of a car: it was either "goddamn good" or "no goddamn good."

Against such a background, it seems remarkable that the Model A turned out to be as good as it did. But it was to Henry's credit that he left such a wide margin for error. The Model A was really over-engineered. Examples now a half-century old have a tightness and integrity one doesn't expect in cars of that age—and possibly any age. Everything from bumper braces to axles to steering column seems twice as strong as it needs to be. The inclusion of standard features like hydraulic shocks, four-wheel mechanical brakes, and safety glass shows that seat-of-the-pants engineering wasn't a bad way to do things, at least in 1926.

The Model A's styling was generally left to Edsel Ford and Hungarian-born engineer Joe Galamb. Galamb was actually the overall technical director for the project, but put a good deal of time into just the body. Because Henry insisted on a gravity-feed fuel tank (he would have nothing to do with fuel pumps, possibly because somebody else owned the patents), Edsel and Galamb had to design the body around it. They gracefully molded the tank into the body cowl—so smoothly that at first glance one wouldn't know it was there. As a whole, the car was neat, trim, even elegant—adjectives no one ever applied to a Model T. Here, Henry paid one of his rare compliments to Edsel: "We've got a pretty good man in my son. He knows style—how a car ought to look."

Today, a seven-month lapse between the announcement and actual appearance of a new model would probably kill all public enthusiasm for it. Not so in the Model A's time. If anything, the delay only whetted the public's appetite. Following a series of tantalizing ads the car debuted on December 2, 1927. America went wild. Fully 25 million people—nearly a quarter of the nation's population—lined up during the first week alone to see this new Ford. Its arrival was compared in importance to news of the World War I armistice. Yet Ford Motor Company had placed only a few ads; it got 90 percent of the publicity absolutely free.

With good looks, lively performance and easy handling, the Model A deserved all the adulation it received. With 10 models and prices ranging from $375 to $600 (the neat town car cost $1200), there was a Model A for everyone. Each offered tremendous value for the money. But as one New York newspaper put it, they were not the Model Ts the nation had grown to love: "The old, black, rusty, cantankerous, obstinate, sputtering Ford brought wisdom to many and made many wise men go raving, tearing mad. This new lily-of-the-valley isn't going to teach us anything. It looks as if it would run indefinitely without complaint, which is all wrong. It is made for serenity and comfort, which is all wrong. Where is the gas tank? Up front where it can be reached. Where is the timer? Up on top where it can no longer bark your knuckles. Where are the brake bands? In a ridiculously exposed position where their value as trainers of character and refined language is completely lost."

Of course, the nation was quite glad to accept all these new "wrong" features. In 1929, after Model A production got going in earnest, Ford returned to first place in the industry with 1.5 million cars against Chevrolet's 950,000. In 1930, despite slackening demand as the Depression set in, it was 1.15 million to 683,000.

These victories were sweet but fleeting. As the Depression wore on, those few who could afford a new car bought more Chevrolets than Fords. Chevy sales in 1931 were almost equal to 1930's, for example, while Ford's fell by 50 percent. Even the arrival of the Ford V-8 in 1932 didn't help Dearborn recapture the top position. In the 1931–40 period, Ford outsold Chevrolet in only one year, 1935.

The Model A changed very little during its four-year life. For 1929 a station wagon was added, priced at only $695, an astonishingly low figure. For 1930, with four million Model As already on the road, the handsome DeLuxe phaeton arrived to grace the lineup. Priced at $625 (against only $440 for the Standard phaeton), this sharp-looking open Ford featured leather upholstery, lefthand-mounted spare tire, and folding trunk rack.

The A put in its final appearance for 1931, but it went out in style. No less than 19 different models were offered, including a new convertible sedan and the close-coupled Victoria coupe with either canvas or steel top. The '31 was easily recognized by a body-color panel set into the top front part of the radiator. Over five million Model As were now on the road.

In car-collecting circles today, the Model A Ford is by far the most popular single model of any make. Two enormous clubs cater to a multitude of owners and fans, and a whole mini-industry sprung up decades ago in reproduction replacement parts, copies of the originals that are accurate to a fault. It is hard to believe that all this enthusiasm surrounds a car that was produced for a mere four years—but then you have to drive a Model A to understand it all. More than anything else on wheels, it kept America mobile at a critical time which, like the Model T, endeared it to so many people. Viewed strictly as a car, it proved that quality was not strictly the province of upper-echelon makes like Packard, Cadillac, and Lincoln. In fact, more people than we realize are probably thinking of the Model A Ford when they mouth that old cliché, "they don't make 'em like they used to."

LeBaron-styled Model A Phaeton, 1930

1931 Model AA Dump Truck

1931 Model A Victoria Coupe

1931 Model A DeLuxe Roadster

1931 Model A DeLuxe Roadster

1934 DeLuxe Roadster

1932-40 Ford V-8:
Henry's Last Masterpiece

There are two ways of viewing the Model 18 Ford V-8—as a car and as a product. Either way, it stands as one of the most important Fords of all time. As a car it was light years ahead of the opposition from the day it went on sale. The reason: its new "monobloc" V-8 engine, which had scads of power and was capable of even more with a few simple bolt-on modifications. As a product it was in a class by itself. The first popularly priced car with V-8 power, it pioneered a whole new approach to automotive marketing, which other makes ultimately followed. It set the stage for the V-8 era that began in earnest after World War II and peaked in the 1960s. And the American industry does nothing better than design and build V-8 engines.

It is important to note these points up front, because it is what the Ford V-8 lacked, rather than what it had, that is usually emphasized in assessing its place in history. For example, it lacked a modern suspension system and hydraulic brakes for a very long time. This put it at a growing technical and commercial disadvantage as time went on. It lacked such features for one reason: Henry Ford didn't like them. And in 1932, Henry was still very much the boss of Ford Motor Company—and would be almost to the day he died 15 years later.

The flathead Ford V-8 engine lasted 21 years, longer than even the Model T. In retrospect, it can certainly be viewed as a good idea for its time, and it remained so throughout its production life. The technical intricacies of this engine are outlined in the following chapter. Suffice it to say here that it was a dramatic upstaging of Chevrolet—exactly what Henry Ford wanted.

The V-8 model was Henry's replacement for his "interim" car, the Model A. Contrary to some accounts, Ford knew even before the Model A went on sale that Chevrolet was brewing a six. The Model A was equipped precisely with the knowledge that the four would be only a temporary measure. Let Chevy go ahead and commit itself; Ford would leapfrog ahead later with two more cylinders. It was just like Henry, and from the standpoint of performance and technology it was exactly the correct strategy. The methods (attributed largely to Charlie Sorensen) that enabled Ford to produce the monobloc engine at a reasonable price were exactly correct, too.

As with the Model A, styling for the V-8 car was handled by Edsel Ford and Joe Galamb. Some observers pointed out the V-8 looked simply like a scaled-down Lincoln, but the basic shape was mainly a development of the Model A's. Wheelbase grew to 106 inches from the A's 103.5 inches. The frame was beefed up, mainly at the central crossmember. Brake drum diameter was increased from 11 to 12 inches. An important breakthrough in the car's styling was Henry's acceptance of the fuel pump. This allowed Edsel and Galamb to place the gas tank at the rear of the V-8 car instead of clumsily (and dangerously) in the cowl as on the Model A. The central instrument panel was Lincoln-inspired, and obviously no cost-cutting was done there. However, a little money was saved on the bumpers, which were fluted pressed steel instead of a two-piece design as on the Model A. Thus, the V-8's body and chassis engineering were evolutionary rather than revolutionary. The genius of it all was that the car could be restyled each year at relatively low cost. Streamlining came first, for 1933, and progressed to the fabulous 1940 model, one of the best styling jobs of all time.

The V-8 shared its looks with 150,000 four-cylinder cars called Model Bs, which were introduced as stop-gaps when the last Model As were sold in the spring of 1932. Although a certain segment of the market indicated it would prefer to stay with four-cylinder Fords, it really didn't amount to much. There was far stronger interest in the V-8, which was scarcely surprising. The new engine developed 65 bhp at 3400 rpm from 221 cubic inches. That was good for a top speed of nearly 80 mph—and make no mistake, this was *fast* for a car in the Chevrolet or Plymouth class. Considering what you got for your money, the V-8 was probably an even greater bargain than the Model A before it: $460 bought a roadster (comparable Chevy price $475). Even the most expensive version, the convertible sedan, cost just $650 (comparable Chevy also $650). Plymouths were more expensive. The V-8 added only about $50 to the price of the equivalent Model B, which made the total only a little higher than that of the 1931 Model A.

The haste with which it was developed and Ford's lack of extensive testing facilities led to problems with the V-8. As a result, Ford failed to take the production lead away from Chevrolet. For example, early engines were notorious oil-burners, cylinder heads often developed cracks, engine mounts loosened up, and ignition troubles were common. Ford met its guarantees and supplied replacement pistons free of charge, but

buyers continued to defect to Chevrolet in 1932–34.

The dashing restyle for 1933 was a big help. The hood was extended back to the windshield, and doors on closed body styles were hinged at the rear. Fenders were beautifully contoured, skirted, and low-dipped in the front. Wheelbase increased to 112 inches while wheel diameter shrank to 17 inches. Most of the early engine bugs were eliminated by now. At 335,000 units, Ford production was up by 100,000 cars that year. Reliability was demonstrated, curiously enough, by enthusiasts who called themselves hot-rodders. Their growing interest in the flathead mill created a strong aftermarket in high-performance parts developed for it. Certainly no one in a hurry would ever pick a Chevy over a Ford. Even John Dillinger wrote Henry to tell him just how much he liked the product—an unbiased plug from Public Enemy No. 1.

The 1934 Ford V-8 had minor styling changes, but retained the same wheelbase, which would last through the end of the decade. New that year were a revised carburetor and manifold that increased output to 85 bhp. Despite design and engineering improvements, Ford kept prices low; you could still buy the two-passenger coupe for a little more than $500 in 1934.

The station wagon body style, which Ford had introduced with the 1929 Model A, continued as part of the V-8 lineup. Wagon bodies were constructed of birch or maple, supplied through 1935 by a company in Kentucky. Henry Ford, who was fascinated with the idea of "growing automobiles" (he invested heavily in soybean product research), decided to eliminate dependence on outside suppliers by setting up his own lumber works in Iron Mountain, Michigan. From 1936 on, this facility provided Ford's wagon bodies, the extensive hardwood forests nearby keeping shipping costs low.

The "round look," exemplified by the 1934 Chrysler Airflow, arrived at Ford for 1935. For the first time sedans were available with a trunk designed as an integral part of the body. Engine improvements included a new camshaft and better crankcase ventilation. Rated horsepower remained at 85, but that was still well ahead of the six-cylinder competition from Chevrolet and Plymouth. The frame and rear axle were strengthened, but Henry stubbornly insisted on retain-

1932 DeLuxe Roadster

1932 DeLuxe 3-Window Coupe

1933 DeLuxe Tudor Sedan

1933 Station Wagon

1935 DeLuxe Convertible Sedan

1935 DeLuxe 3-Window Coupe

1934 DeLuxe 3-Window Coupe

1936 DeLuxe 3-Window Coupe

ing the transverse-leaf front and rear suspension system and mechanical brakes. These aging chassis features definitely weighed against Ford, but not enough to matter. In 1935, for the first time since the height of the Model A, Ford outproduced Chevrolet, 9.5 cars to 8.

For 1936, the hood became longer and more pointed, and the grille was given a sharper V-shape. Henry had been convinced to part with wire wheels in favor of pressed-steel wheels in 1935, so that remnant of the past was gone. A five-passenger cabriolet was added to the lineup, which now totaled 19 Standard and DeLuxe models. The more stylish body types, like the convertibles and roadsters, were offered only in DeLuxe trim. The highest-priced Ford that year was the convertible sedan at $780.

For the previous 10 years, Henry Ford had resolutely resisted the idea of a six-cylinder model. When Edsel and Sorensen pitched for a lower-priced companion line for 1937, Henry again insisted that it have V-8 power. It did. The new engine was smaller, 136 cubic inches, and yielded only 60 horsepower. It had mainly been intended for the European market, where car tax was often based on bore but not stroke. As a result, the "V-8/60," as it was known, had a much-reduced bore—2.6 instead of 3.1 inches. The "V-8/85," meanwhile, received a relocated water pump, larger insert

bearings, and new cast alloy-steel pistons. The V-8/60 was never a great success in the American market, but it wasn't until 1941 that it was replaced by a more logical inline six.

Important advances were made in body design for the '37 models. All-steel construction eliminated the cloth inserts previously used on roofs of closed body styles. Streamlining became more evident as headlamps were integrated into the front fenders and the grille (now with a thin horizontal-bar motif) was stretched back. In a year of generally questionable styling, the '37 Ford was a standout—proof that streamlining didn't have to mean oddball looks.

Edsel Ford was now company president, but Henry was still very much the boss—and nobody ever restyled Henry. The wizard who had given the world the production line and the Model T, the five-dollar day and the Model A, was a hardened old man by this time, and more stubborn than ever. Adamantly standing in the breech against unionization, he employed a strong-arm lieutenant, one Harry Bennett, to resist the organizing efforts of the United Auto Workers. In 1937, men distributing union handbills took a brutal beating from Bennett's troops, and Henry's public image suffered. A stroke in 1938 seemed to make his attitudes only more inflexible.

The old man's reliance on Bennett, whose advice he often accepted over his son's, took its toll on the sensitive Edsel, who died before his time in 1943. With him passed one of the industry's great leaders, a man whose accomplishments might have equalled his father's had he lived long enough. Ford Motor Company's fortunes declined during the late '30s and early '40s. It was not until 1945 when Henry Ford II, Edsel's son, arrived as president that the decline was halted—and then only just in time.

Continued reliance on outmoded design ideas was no help to Ford sales in 1938, a recession year that saw industry volume sink by 50 percent. The standard Ford picked up styling features from the previous year's DeLuxe, and the upper series was restyled. The roadster body type had already disappeared, and the phaeton was making its last stand. (Typically, Ford was late in realizing the obvious: Plymouth's last roadsters and phaetons were built in 1932, Chevy's in 1935.)

DeLuxe models were again restyled for 1939 with a vertical stainless-steel grille, clean front fenders, and flush headlamps. Prices were up only $5 model for model. Mechanical changes included a column-mounted gearshift and—at last—hydraulic brakes, three years after Chevrolet and 11 years after Plymouth. (Transverse leaf springs, though, still supported Ford chassis, and would through 1948.) Though late in the game, a memorable model was in the wings: the fabulous '40.

The '40 Ford has become unequivocally the most desirable flathead V-8 model in the engine's 21-year history, and rightly so. Its styling, the work of Bob Gregorie guided by the brilliant Edsel Ford, was beyond reproach. The hood was crisply pointed, and tapered toward the front to meet a handsome horizontal-bar grille. The headlamps (sealed-beams for the first time) were faired into smooth chrome fender nacelles. The fenders were elegantly curved to complement the shapely body. The rear ones often wore skirts, which enhanced the streamlined overall appearance.

The V-8/60 was in its final season, offered only in coupes and sedans. The V-8/85 was available in a wide range of both Standard- and DeLuxe-trim models. Top of the line was the $849 convertible coupe—today recognized as one of the classic prewar designs, and one of the most sought-after Fords. Despite all this, Ford would still not outsell Chevrolet (which was also instituting design improvements) this year, and wouldn't until 1957.

Although the flathead engine had over a decade of production ahead of it in 1940, the cars it would power through 1948 would be less impressive than the 1932–40 models. They were heavier and clumsier in appearance, with little of the elegance found in the 1933, 1937, or 1940 designs. Interesting body styles like the roadster and convertible sedan had disappeared, and technically the engine was rapidly becoming outmoded. But we can say that, through 1940 at least, Dearborn was still producing exceptional cars. And if their place in our memory is an indication, that judgment is not likely to change.

1937 DeLuxe 5-Window Coupe

1938 DeLuxe Fordor Sedan

1939 DeLuxe Fordor Sedan

1939 DeLuxe Convertible Coupe

1940 DeLuxe Convertible Coupe

Ford's Flathead V-8: Long-Distance Runner

$\mathscr{L}$ong before Chevrolet introduced its six-cylinder models in 1929, Ford had been experimenting with a variety of engine designs. Such experiments had, in fact, been going on since 1913 in a private laboratory Henry Ford had set up next to his home. But that work led only to engines for marine and farm tractor use. Meanwhile, the four-cylinder Model T carried on as usual.

Ford's experience with the V-8 configuration began in 1922 when the firm acquired Henry Leland's Lincoln Motor Company. At about the same time, Edsel Ford and his brother-in-law, Ernest Kanzler, realized that the Model T could not go on forever. Edsel insisted that what Ford needed was a six—and he was right. The low-priced Saxon Six had been a sales winner in 1915–20. Durant's Flint and Hudson's Essex moved to six cylinders in 1924, followed by Willys's Whippet in 1926 and Studebaker's Erskine in 1927. On order from Edsel, engineers Laurence Sheldrick and Eugene Farkas began studies and tests for a new six in 1923. Several prototype engines were installed in Model Ts, but every one proposed for production was rejected for one reason or another.

Meanwhile, Henry Ford had become infatuated with the X-engine concept suggested to him by Allan Horton (who left Ford in 1924). This was an air-cooled radial design with two rows of four cylinders arranged in a cross or "X" formation. The result was a very compact, lightweight, and well-balanced package. Henry like it so much he had Farkas and Sheldrick pulled off the six-cylinder experiments, along with Harold Hicks. The X-engine was road-tested in an Oldsmobile, not a Model T, chassis, hooked to the Tin Lizzy's two-speed planetary transmission. But development stalled as the reports came in, each more negative than the one before it. Nevertheless, Henry refused to give up.

Edsel temporarily distracted his father by insisting on an improved, enlarged four for the Model A. Farkas and Sheldrick designed and developed it. Then the Chevy Six appeared. While Edsel wanted to revive the six-cylinder program, Henry refused, perhaps from a vague feeling that it would be taken as an admission that he had been wrong and Chevrolet had been right. That was when talk began of a V-8, which immediately got Henry's full support. Not content with the company's Lincoln experience, Henry ordered his engineers to study every V-8 on the market. So, Ford Motor Company bought a Cadillac, a Cunningham, a Peerless, and even an older Wills Sainte Claire from a used-car dealer, and took them apart.

What it found in these engines were two separate four-cylinder blocks on a common crankcase, construction that would be too costly for the low-priced Ford. So, Henry ordered the block and crankcase cast as a single unit, and threw the problem of how to do it to Charlie Sorensen and Joseph Galamb. Galamb, who had engineered the transmission for the Model T, came up with a structure that Sorensen determined could be manufactured in Ford's customarily huge volume and at the right price. Major specifications came directly from Henry, with Farkas and Sheldrick assisting him. The first fully detailed drawings were made by Carl Schultz and Don Sullivan in May 1930, and prototypes were on the road that summer. By November a revised version was ready. Another batch of test engines was made up, perhaps 25 or 30. Some went on the dynamometer, others went into cars, and the rest went to the laboratory for evaluation of lower-cost parts. The new V-8 proved outstandingly powerful for its size, and no major problems were found. But the decision to produce it, as always, rested with Henry, who finally made up his mind on December 7th, 1931. After that, the race was on to bring it out as quickly as possible, so tooling and production planning activities were hectic.

Production began at the River Rouge plant on March 9th, 1932, and the Ford V-8 was in dealers' showrooms on the last day of that month. It was America's first and only V-8 car priced below $500 (the range was $460–$650 depending on body style). It should be noted that

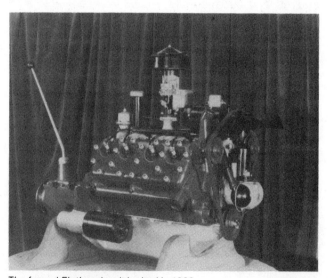

The famed Flathead as it looked in 1932

the V-8 was not originally intended to replace the four-cylinder Model B engine altogether. Rather, it was to have been an extra-cost option, Henry's way of hedging his bet. But he needn't have worried. The V-8 was an instant hit. By the end of 1933, Ford stopped building four-cylinder passenger cars.

Weighing 512 pounds, the V-8 delivered 65 bhp at 3400 rpm, compared to 596 pounds for the Chevy six, which also produced 65 bhp but at 2800 rpm. With its larger displacement (221 vs. 207 cubic inches) the Ford engine was less stressed than the Chevy six, and generated more torque where it counted. Simplicity was the keynote of its design. The cylinder banks were angled at 90 degrees to each other. Primary imbalance forces were eliminated by the use of a two-plane crankshaft, only 20 inches long, which ran in three white-metal main bearings. Connecting rods worked side by side, two per crankpin journal. The cylinder axes were offset 0.1875-inch from the crankshaft center to reduce side thrust on the pistons. The top end had a typical L-head layout with a single camshaft mounted in the valley between the two cylinder banks. The heads were aluminum castings, and gave a compression ratio of 4.6:1. A cast-iron manifold provided a base for a tall, one-barrel downdraft carburetor that towered above the engine.

In its rush to get the V-8 to market, Ford hadn't allowed sufficient development time, so the early engines were far from trouble-free. Oil consumption tended to be high, a problem traced to the piston rings. The ignition system acted up, too. There was a high incidence of water-pump malfunctions, and the engine mount locations tended to feed engine vibration through the frame to the passenger compartment. Most of these defects were corrected during 1933. When the 1934 models came out, the V-8 was fully satisfactory. The '34 version even included a major innovation: cast iron replaced forged steel for the crankshaft, slashing the cost of that part.

For 1933, compression was boosted to 5.5:1, raising power output to 75 bhp at 3800 rpm. The following year, 6.33:1 compression and a two-barrel downdraft carb with two-level manifold pushed peak power to 85 bhp. The V-8/85 was on its way to fame. Ford produced its millionth V-8 in June 1934, and the two millionth just one year later. By this time, Ford had enough confidence in the flathead to supply engines to Harry Miller for four highly experimental front-wheel-drive Indy racers entered at the Speedway in 1935. None of them went the full distance, however, due to inadequate testing and preparation.

Ford's European subsidiaries were becoming increasingly interested in the V-8, but needed a smaller version. That was because of high horsepower tax in some countries (based on displacement in Germany and France, on cylinder bore and number in Great Britain) and higher gasoline prices. Out of this came the V-8/60, for which Don Sullivan was the principal design engineer. The basic layout of the V-8/85 was retained, but cylinder dimensions were reduced (bore from 3.062 to 2.60 inches, stroke from 3.75 to 3.20 inches) for a displacement of 136 cubic inches. This unit went into production at Cologne, Germany; Dagenham, England; and Asnieres, France in 1936. The following year it was added to the production program in Dearborn. The U.S. version had a 6.6:1 compression ratio and delivered 60 bhp at 3500 rpm. Though it was discontinued for the U.S. in 1941, it was built through the war years in Britain and France for military use. Allied bombing halted German production in 1944. After the war, the V-8/60 was revived for the British Ford Pilot starting in 1947 and the French Ford Vedette in 1949.

Returning to the V-8/85, it was redesigned for 1937 —so much so that Ford experts considered it virtually all-new. There were no internal changes, but the water pump was moved from the front of the head to the bottom of the block. In this way it no longer drew hot water out of the engine but pushed cold water into it, effectively ending the cooling problems. For smoother running the engine mount system was revised with new biscuit-type mounts, two at the front of the engine and two at the rear of the transmission. Also, the aluminum cylinder heads were replaced by cheaper cast-iron ones.

When the Mercury was being prepared in 1937–38, it was decided the new medium-priced model must have more power than the cheaper Ford. Accordingly, the V-8 was bored out to 3.375-inch, giving 239.4 cid. On a 6.75:1 compression ratio, this engine delivered 95 bhp at 3800 rpm for 1939.

When car production resumed after World War II, the 221-cid Ford unit was rated at 90 bhp and the Mercury version at 100 bhp. Both were favorites of hot-rod mechanics and builders of special cars everywhere despite their old-fashioned side-valve layout and restricted porting. Zora Arkus-Duntov, later to win fame as the "father" of the Corvette, was an independent operator in those days, and saw a ready market for a more modern head design for these engines. His Ardun conversion offered splayed overhead valves above hemispherical combustion chambers. Ardun heads were just what the hop-up artists had been looking for. They even found their way into a production car, the British-built Allard, many of which relied on Ford power. But by the end of the '40s the old V-8 was finished, and Ford Motor Company knew it. In 1946–47 a whole new team was beginning to reshape the company, and an overhead-valve replacement for the famous flathead was one of the results. It came none too soon.

After a long 21-year production run, Ford phased out the flathead. Appropriately, its last automotive application was in the Golden Anniversary 1953 Ford models. Yet even though it had outlived its usefulness, it was an engine that had served Ford faithfully and well. Beyond that, it brought the power and refinement of much more expensive cars to the low-priced field, and provided a marketing incentive for other manufacturers that eventually led to the modern, high-compression V-8s of the '50s and '60s. Few engines have been as influential— or more fondly remembered.

1946 Sportsman Convertible

1946-48 Sportsman: A Touch of Class

As the '30s passed and the '40s momentously entered, Ford Motor Company was in a precarious position. The company had steadily lost sales ground over the previous five years, its sprightly V-8 notwithstanding, and now found itself third in the industry behind GM and Chrysler. What would have happened under the flawed leadership of an aged Henry Ford in a peacetime 1941–45 will never be known, however. Germany had invaded Poland on September 1, 1939.

At the outbreak of war in Europe, Henry still adhered steadfastly to the beliefs he had espoused for a lifetime. He firmly allied himself with Lindbergh and the "American Firsters," declaring that the United States must not be drawn into the conflict. But the United States, as Churchill said, could not escape world responsibility. After Pearl Harbor, Henry told production chief Charles Sorensen to clear the decks for defense work. He built the great bomber factory at Willow Run, and turned the enormous power of the Rouge plant toward his country's needs in its most perilous hour.

Sadly, the war years saw the untimely death of Henry's son Edsel and the departure of the brilliant designers who had gravitated to him. One by one, but in rapid succession, they left—Sheldrick, Wilbel, Gregorie. Their loss, wrote historians Allan Nevins and Frank E. Hill in *Ford: Decline and Rebirth,* were "body blows to the Ford Motor Company."

Into the breech left by the loss of Edsel and his team came two determined and ruthless men—Charles Sorensen and Henry's crony, bodyguard, and all-around "iron man," Harry Bennett. Henry soon decided that Sorensen had to go. "Cast Iron Charlie" was told about it through intermediaries. He had become too ambitious; he wanted to succeed Henry as president; Henry would not have it. Sorensen departed in March 1944. His dramatic dismissal would be compared to that of William S. Knudsen before him and, later, to the firing of Ernest Breech and Lee Iacocca by Henry Ford II.

With Sorensen out, the way seemed clear for Bennett. But the optimistic Bennett hadn't counted on the well-knit family that still controlled the Ford Motor Company (and would for many years to follow). Clara Ford, ever the supportive wife, was equally the only person willing to tell Henry he was wrong. He must now resign, she told him, in favor of his grandson, Henry II. The old man, wrote Nevins and Hill, "was peevishly reluctant." The scales were tipped by Mrs. Edsel Ford, who took Clara's side: "If this is not done," she announced, "I shall sell my stock." Henry capitulated.

In August 1945, Henry Ford II, still in uniform, was summoned to Fair Lane, his grandfather's Dearborn estate. There, the elder Henry said he was ready to step aside. HF II knew what he was up against. "I told him I'd take it only if I had a completely free hand to make any changes I wanted to make," he said. "We argued about that—but he didn't withdraw his offer."

Henry Ford submitted his resignation as president on September 20th. The Board of Directors accepted it the next day, and named Henry Ford II to replace him. Harry Bennett left the company that day, with the window-dressing of a one-month directorship. Angrily he had told the new president, "You're taking over a billion-dollar organization here that you haven't contributed a thing to!"

Henry II was about to start contributing. By bringing new, young, talented people into the organization, he would turn its fortunes around in less than a decade and make Ford a near rival to mighty General Motors.

As World War II drew to a close, most U.S. automakers faced a dilemma. Should they get back into volume production quickly with warmed-over prewar models, or should they put the rush on all-new postwar designs? Studebaker, after a brief run of 1942 lookalikes labeled 1946s, did the latter. Most everyone else did the former. Henry Ford II had no choice. His company, though financed to the tune of nearly $700 million, was heavily in debt, and faced the massive cost of winding down its war machine. Above all, Ford needed to get back into civilian production: the road back was going to be a long one.

The Ford Sportsman and its second cousin, the Mercury Sportsman, were the first product decisions made by the new man in charge. He reasoned that if the first postwar Fords couldn't be all-new, at least some of them could be strikingly different on the surface— enough to lure buyers into newly reopened showrooms. Paneling convertibles in maple or yellow birch with mahogany-veneer inserts seemed like a pretty good way to do that.

Before his departure, styling director Bob Gregorie had designed a convertible of this sort, and HF II liked it. Furthermore, the company already had a massive timber forest and a processing plant up at Iron Mountain, Michigan. This operation had supplied raw materials for building station wagon bodies since 1936, so there was no lack of wood. And because the panels could be grafted easily right onto the existing Ford convertible body, building such a car would be no more difficult than turning out woodie wagons. This is not to imply that the Sportsman's panels were mere appliqués. They were, in fact, structural body elements made from solid wood blocks and mitered together with handcrafted precision.

Wood is nature's product, not man's, so no two Sportsmans were exactly alike. Three different types of wood were used during the production run. Style "A," according to Sportsman enthusiast Dr. Thomas B. Garrett, "had horizontal pieces running full length across the doors and quarters. In the 'B' and 'C' styles, the full-length members ran vertically from top to bottom. All 1946 Sportsmans used the 'A' panels whereas '47s were divided between all three." (Ford lists only

1947 Super DeLuxe Station Wagon

28 Sportsmans for the 1948 model year, all actually reserialed 1947s.)

Incidentally, the woodie conversion had a problem—the production 1946 rear fenders. They wrapped around too much at the rear, which would have cut into the wooden trunklid. The solution was to use fenders (complete with taillights) from the 1941 sedan delivery. Sportsman body panels from the cowl forward were shared with other Ford models. The car was offered only with the L-head V-8 engine, not the Ford six, and hydraulic window lifts and vanity mirrors on both sun-visors were included as standard equipment.

Ella Raines, the Hollywood actress, took delivery of the first Sportsman on Christmas Day 1945, a scant eight weeks after Henry Ford II had assumed the presidency. Despite only incidental publicity, the model was a fair success considering that it cost $800 more than the V-8 Fordor sedan and $500 more than the standard all-steel convertible. A total of 3487 were built for the three model years plus 205 of the longer-wheelbase Mercury Sportsman, offered only for 1946.

The significance of the handsome Sportsman is not so much its qualities as a car as its mission of luring prospective buyers back to Ford dealerships. Most who did buy, of course, drove out in one of the plain-Jane sedans. The Sportsman's objective was to add a touch of class to an otherwise very ordinary group of 1946–48 models based on prewar tooling.

Performance was not one of the Sportsman's assets. It weighed about 100 pounds more than the standard convertible and 200 pounds more than the Fordor sedan. It had the flathead V-8 and moved along well, but wasn't sensationally quick. The typical Sportsman would do about 85 mph maximum and run the 0–60 mph dash in a bit less than 20 seconds. Definitely an understeerer, the Sportsman had adequate handling for a car riding antediluvean transverse leaf springs front and rear. It still copes well with today's roads and traffic conditions including 55-mph freeways. Most examples are unusually solid for convertibles, testifying to their very careful construction. Altogether, the Sportsman is an entertaining piece of transportation—and certainly the most noteworthy production Ford of the early postwar years.

Ford wasn't the only manufacturer to doll up a standard car with wood trim. The Chrysler Town & Country appeared in sedan and convertible form at about the same time. Ditto the Nash Suburban, a wood-embellished Ambassador sedan that actually cost less than the Sportsman. The Town & Country was really in a class by itself—longer, heavier, more expensive, and more luxurious than the others. In a drag race between these non-wagon woodies, the Sportsman would lead the field due to its comparatively lower weight and its strong V-8.

All the postwar woodie specials are avidly sought-after today. Considerable research has yielded reliable "survival figures" on these models, though the odds are low you'll find one for sale. It is estimated that about 300 of the true Town & Countrys survive, counting the later versions based on the restyled 1949–50 bodyshell. Out of the 100 Nash Suburbans built, however, no more than a dozen are known to exist. Ford Sportsman enthusiasts have about 100 of their snappy ragtops to scout out, again not very many. The most spectacular find would be a Mercury Sportsman: currently there are only three or four of them still left.

In April 1947, as the last Sportsman rolled off the line and his company looked toward a brighter future, Henry Ford died. Despite the bitterness and disappointment in his last years, his achievements remained untarnished. He established his company in 1903 purely on venture capital and an idea. He had taken just five years to produce a mechanical device that enabled a nation to conquer its vast size. No geographically large country had ever before built a world-class economy; for her's America was in his debt. No less important were his production innovations like the high-volume assembly line and the five-dollar work day; product advances like the brilliant, yet simple and reliable, Model A; and engineering benchmarks like the monobloc V-8, which pioneered a whole new approach to affordable transportation.

If there was ever a "folk hero" to come from the ranks of the automobile industry, Henry Ford surely was one. Along with Edison, Firestone, and the Wright brothers, he was an inspiration for millions—a symbol of the dreams, drive, and inventiveness that sparked America's unparalleled growth and prosperity. For a man who once remarked "history is bunk," Henry Ford certainly did more than enough to earn a permanent place in it.

1946 Sportsman Convertible

1946 Super DeLuxe Fordor Sedan

1947 Super DeLuxe Convertible

1951 Custom Tudor Sedan

1949~51:
The Postwar Renaissance

During Henry Ford II's first two years as Ford Motor Company president the firm's losses ran as high as $10 million a month. Young Henry was amazed— and appalled—at the business methods he found in use. One department figured out how much business it had done at the end of a day by weighing the paperwork!

The 27-year-old auto chief began looking for help. Late in 1945 he found it in an unexpected place: Litton Industries. Litton chairman Tex Thornton had written Ford to offer the services of himself and a group of talented young officers just being discharged from the Air Force. To Thornton's surprise, Henry accepted. Thornton's people became the nucleus of the "Whiz Kids," the bright managerial team which would turn Ford's fortunes around. Then, in early 1946, HF II coaxed Ernest R. Breech to Dearborn from the Bendix Division of General Motors. Breech served as his right hand until he was unexpectedly fired in 1959.

Along with GM and Chrysler, Ford would completely overhaul all its car lines for 1949—its first all-new postwar models. Designs for the new Lincoln and Mercury had been laid down by Bob Gregorie before he'd departed during the war. The '49 Ford assignment was handed to two key men: engineering vice-president Harold Youngren, a recent arrival from Oldsmobile and a Breech recruit, and design consultant George W. Walker. Youngren initially envisioned two Ford lines: the standard 114-inch-wheelbase car that ultimately emerged and a 97-inch-wheelbase front-wheel-drive compact (which was eventually built by Ford of France as the Vedette).

Although both Ford engines would stay the same (an ohv V-8 would come, but not until 1954), the rest of the 1949 specification was completely different from '48. It was probably the most changed Ford since the Model A had replaced the Model T a generation before.

Wheelbase was not changed, but every other dimension was. The '49 was three inches lower and fractionally shorter and narrower than the '48, though its new, flush-fender styling gave it a much sleeker appearance. Despite the more compact body, Youngren's people managed to increase seat width by half a foot, find more legroom, maintain headroom, and create a much larger luggage compartment. Although the new car seemed more spacious as a result, careful attention to detail brought it in at the targeted curb weight of under 3000 pounds; only the convertible and woodie wagon were slighty heavier. By contrast, no 1948 Ford tipped the scales under 3000 pounds, and some were over 3500. Less weight made the '49 livelier despite the carryover engines.

The new car was also dramatically different underneath in a way that probably would have upset the elder Henry Ford. His traditional beam front axle and transverse-leaf-spring suspension were gone. In their place were an independent front suspension acting

1949 Custom Tudor Sedan

1949 Custom Station Wagon

1949 Custom Station Wagon

1950 Custom Crestliner Tudor Sedan

1950 Custom Convertible

through coil springs and wishbones, and longitudinal leaf springs used to locate the rear axle. Final drive was now of the hypoid, instead of spiral-bevel, type, and torque-tube drive was replaced by Hotchkiss. The transmission was completely re-engineered, and the old two-speed rear axle gave way to a modern optional overdrive. (Ford-O-Matic, the new automatic then under development, did not arrive until 1951. Ford had tried without success to purchase Studebaker's automatic for the '49 models.) The redesigned brakes were given greater swept area. All these new components were hung onto an up-to-date ladder-type frame that replaced the heavy X-member frame on all models except the convertible.

The '49 was so desperately needed that Henry Ford II personally told development engineer Bill Burnett to forget last-minute efforts to reduce noise, and to concentrate instead on the remaining problem of front-end geometry caused by the engine's extreme forward location. According to *Special-Interest Autos* magazine, however, the engineers "kept right on improving the car after introduction, insulating it, changing the fan pitch, the camshaft, body mounts, and exhaust system for less noise." By the time the similar-looking '50 model debuted, they had made it a very quiet automobile.

There are several conflicting claims as to who deserves the credit for the 1949–51 design, which was presented to management in final form by styling consultant George Walker. Walker had instituted a crash program among all his assistants, who produced at least a dozen different proposals. The one accepted was that of Richard Caleal, a freelance stylist working for Walker and previously associated with the Loewy team at Studebaker. Caleal worked so hard to sell his car to Walker that friends nicknamed him "the Persian rug salesman."

Caleal's shape was clean if slab-sided. Only recently has it been learned that he was strongly influenced by Loewy concepts. Facing a tight deadline, Caleal asked his former associates, Bob Bourke and Holden Koto, to help him perfect the clay model for Walker. Remembers Bourke: "The final clay model was baked in Dick Caleal's wife's oven in Mishawaka, Indiana, greatly affecting the quality of cuisine in the Caleal household for months. Our influence was the bullet-nose grille, which was similar to the component on Studebaker front ends for 1950–51." Caleal's model was approved with hardly a change. Walker did turn its vertical taillights horizontally and gave them accenting "pods" that ran forward along the rear fenders to add visual interest to the slab sides.

The '49 Ford was an expensive program for a company only just recovering from some pretty lean years. It took 10 million man hours and $72 million just to get it into production. Its debut date was moved up to June 1948, because Ford literally could not afford to wait for the usual fall introduction. But the effort paid off handsomely, and Ford recorded a gratifying $177 million profit for calendar year 1949. And it bested Chevy in actual model year production by over 100,000 units.

But a few things were left undone on the '49 Ford.

Ford's first hardtop: 1951 Victoria

1951 Custom Victoria Hardtop

1951 Country Squire Station Wagon

1951 DeLuxe Business Coupe

The tremendous tooling costs left no money for launching a hardtop convertible until 1951. Walker's staff, however, came up with an interim solution in the Crestliner for 1950. Based on the Tudor sedan bodyshell, it offered a hardtop's sporty style without a pillarless roof. Its looks were influenced by Gordon M. Buehrig, famed designer of the prewar Auburns and Duesenbergs. Buehrig, who would also create the first true Ford hardtop, likened the Crestliner's two-tone side styling to the classic "LeBaron sweep" of the custombody era.

The Crestliner bowed late in the season as the top offering in the upper-level Custom (V-8) series. It sold for $1711, $200 more than the Custom Tudor (though its 1951 price was cut to $1595, only $90 higher). In addition to the vivid color sweep it sported a padded vinyl-covered roof, anodized-gold fender nameplates, and a luxurious color-keyed interior. Despite the late start, Crestliner sales were a respectable 17,601.

For 1951, the third and last edition of the Caleal design, the Crestliner was joined by a genuine pillarless hardtop, and sales dropped to 8703. All the '51 Fords had a new face courtesy of a thick horizontal grille bar with two smaller bullets at its outboard ends instead of one large central bullet. Inside was a handsomely redesigned asymmetrical dashboard. Except

for the addition of optional Ford-O-Matic Drive, there were no mechanical changes. Customs retained the classic flathead monobloc V-8 with 100 bhp; the cheaper Deluxe models continued with Ford's 95-bhp, 226-cid flathead six.

Buehrig's hardtop was christened the Victoria, and, like the Crestliner, was available only in Custom V-8 trim. Response to its dashing appearance and plush interior was enormous compared to Crestliner sales: 110,286 Victorias were sold, a figure that beat both the Chevrolet Bel Air (103,356) and Plymouth's Belvedere (about 30,000) in the battle of the low-priced hardtops.

The Victoria's sales performance, and a surge in hardtop sales throughout the industry, made it unnecessary to continue the Crestliner after 1951. However, the model has since gained collector status, and is widely sought-after today. Its rakish two-toning (in arresting color combinations like black with yellow or maroon) made it a striking addition to the Ford line. Together with the 1951 Victoria and, of course, the 1949–51 convertibles, the Crestliner is among the most desirable Fords of the first postwar generation. Unlike the inelegant products of 1946–48, these cars showed Ford was well on the road to recovery. And with the Fords that would come in the future, the trip wouldn't take long.

1954 Crestline Skyliner

1954~56
Skyliner & Crown Victoria: Roof With a View

𝓘n 1951, Ford Motor Company again outproduced Chrysler Corporation to regain second place among the world's automobile manufacturers. It held on to second for the rest of the '50s and throughout the '60s. Considering that Dearborn had only three makes to Chrysler's and GM's five, that sales performance was remarkable. Much of it was due to the success of the Ford line. Lincoln was never a match for Cadillac, and Mercury had to contend with the combined might of Pontiac, Oldsmobile, and Buick from GM and Chrysler, Dodge, and DeSoto from Highland Park. Edsel, Ford's reinforcement in the medium-priced field for 1958, was a failure, and was dropped early in the 1960 model year.

One of the reasons Ford Division did so well in these years was that it never seemed to stop running out of good ideas. The Sportsman, the new 1949 line, the Crestliner, and the Victoria hardtop were the first of these after the war. The 1954 Skyliner and the 1955–56 Crown Victoria were two more. Together with the companion Mercury Sun Valley, these Fords had something that had previously been seen only in show cars—a see-through top.

Designers began thinking about "bubbletops" in the '30s, when plastic began to be accepted as a structural as well as decorative material. The first such application was by John Tjaarda for Briggs, a one-piece plastic top for a 1939 Plymouth convertible sedan. Even before the end of World War II, half a dozen manufacturers titillated the public with promises that see-through cars would be the wave of the future in the postwar years.

Hardened veterans scoffed at the idea. When Henry Kaiser, the wartime shipbuilding magnate, promised to build such a car once peace returned, his soon-to-be-partner, Joseph W. Frazer (then president of Graham-Paige) cracked, "I think the public is being misled by all these pictures of plastic models with glass tops, done by artists who probably wouldn't want to sit under those tops and sweat." He called Kaiser's notion "about as half-baked as some of his other ideas." Later, Frazer was happy to take Kaiser (and his bottomless money bag) as a partner, and Kaiser-Frazer built cars for 10 years. But it never built a bubbletop production model, and neither did anyone else—until Ford.

Impetus for the Skyliner was probably helped by the arrival of Gordon Buehrig. Buehrig had come to Ford to design the Crestliner and Victoria, and would later play a role in developing the beautiful 1956 Continental Mark II. He had previously worked with Raymond Loewy, a leading proponent of the see-through top. As a freelance designer, Buehrig had created the stillborn TASCO car, which had hinged transparent plastic roof sections, an idea he patented. He was later moved to take issue with General Motors when it showed something similar on an experimental Corvette. "But I settled," he said. "They were too big to sue."

A forecast of the Skyliner was seen in the XL-500 experimental car, a 1953 exercise featuring a clear plastic top bisected by a forward-leaning center pillar that wrapped up and over the roof. In 1955, the same idea appeared on the Mystere show car where the pillar served as the only structural roof member.

Ford's production bubbletopper was considerably less radical, of course. The Skyliner was essentially a 1954 Crestline Victoria hardtop with a see-through Plexiglass roof insert forward of the "B-pillars." With standard six-cylinder engine, the Skyliner was priced at $2164, $109 more than the normal steel-topped Victoria. Aside from the top and minor identifying trim, the two models were virtually identical.

Ford described the Skyliner in rather flowery prose, claiming for it "a freshness of view, a new gaiety and glamor, vast new areas of visibility, a whole new concept of light and luxury . . . you're comfortably 'out of doors' all year long . . . with that wonderful feeling of being fashionably first." This happy puffery wasn't entirely accurate. To reduce heat and glare, Ford tinted the Plexiglas section green, which made for a kind of bilious interior ambience that was more than a little weird. *Motor Trend* magazine's Walt Woron quipped: "It may cause many a young lady to check her makeup. She might as well switch to green lipstick."

Joe Frazer's old fear about passengers sweating (remember, air conditioning was not common at the time) proved at least partly true. Though desert tests claimed only a five-degree difference in interior temperature between the Skyliner and the standard Victoria, Ford nevertheless offered a snap-on interior shade. This made the Skyliner at least reasonably practical—and comfortable—for times when the sun was overbearing.

Without its bubbletop, the Skyliner would have been just another car. But Ford styling and engineering were exceptional in the early '50s. The 1952–54 design was restrained for the period—taut, tight, and lean, tastefully executed, and functional. The monobloc engine was finally replaced for 1954 by a first-rate modern V-8, the oversquare, overhead-valve "Y-block" unit. This fine new powerplant stemmed from a project

1952 Crestline Sunliner Convertible

1953 Crestline Fordor Sedan

1954 Crestline Skyliner Hardtop

1954 Skyliner accessory sunshade

started in 1949. Though it displaced the same 239.4 cubic inches, it developed 130 bhp instead of the flathead's 110. The Y-block was also capable of being greatly enlarged. The very next year it was: to 272 cubic inches.

According to Ford engineers, the new V-8 exhibited no valve bounce at all below 5500 rpm. Hard tappets, full-pressure-lubricated rocker arms, umbrella-type valve guides, and dampening coils on valve-spring ends contributed to quiet running and low oil consumption. The combustion chambers followed the Ricardo principle in being shaped like a kidney, with the larger end away from the spark plug. Combustion began in the larger area progressing to the smaller, where gases were cooled by contact with the head and piston. It was quite a contrast to the Chrysler hemi-head V-8 and its symmetrical combustion chambers.

For 1955, Ford revived the old Crestliner idea of a sporty car based on a two-door sedan. This was the Crown Victoria, the work of L. David Ashe, a young designer working under chief stylist Frank Hershey who had created the X-100 and Mystere show cars. These undoubtedly inspired the "Crown Vicky's" roof treatment. A wide chrome band raked forward from bottom to top concealed the B-pillar, and wrapped up onto the roof and down the other side. Though the band looked like a rollbar, it didn't act like one, and engineer Harold Youngren thought enough of the car's body flex to specify the stiffer X-braced frame from the Ford convertible. Consequently, the Crown Victoria was very tight and solid-feeling. A Plexiglas roof section, like the Skyliner's, was available as an option in place of steel forward of the band. As before, it was ¼-inch thick. As the star in 1955's new Fairlane series, the Crown Victoria was usually fully equipped and painted in bright two-tone color schemes. It added zest to an already very impressive Ford line.

Although the plain Crown Victoria had appeal, the plastic-top version didn't: only 1999 were built against 33,165 steel-topped models. In 1956, the idea seemed to be dead. Of only 9812 Crown Victorias built just 603 had the plastic roof. Price was not the deciding factor, for the difference was only $70. What caught up with the bubbletop was its impracticality. Air conditioning was uncommon and very expensive; in a Ford it seemed almost an excess. So, it was the heat that built up inside a non-air-conditioned Skyliner that was without doubt the biggest factor against its success. Joe Frazer had been right all along.

Of course, the basic concept was a good one, and, as such things often do, it later returned in a slightly different form. Today's counterparts to the Skyliner are the glass moonroof and flip-open sunroof. With air conditioning nearly universal now, plus everthing we've learned about glass and plastics in the intervening 30 years, heat is no longer the problem it was in the Skyliner. Thus, the Plexi-topped Skyliner/Crown Victoria will go down as great cars from Ford—lesser greats, perhaps, but cars that nevertheless started a new trend that would ultimately prove popular.

1954	Production	Price (Six/V-8)
Crestline Skyliner	13,344	$2164/2241
1955		
Crown Victoria Skyliner	1,999	$2202/2302
1956		
Crown Victoria Skyliner	603	$2407/2507

Fairlane Crown Victoria, new for '55

1955 Fairlane Crown Victoria

1955 Crown Victoria with Plexiglas roof

1956 Crown Victoria

Wood prototype for 1955 Thunderbird

1955-57 Thunderbird: Dearborn Dynamite

By the mid-'50s, Ford Motor Company's fortunes had improved dramatically. This encouraged management to begin taking on General Motors product-for-product. Wherever a market gap existed, Ford moved to fill it. For example, in the late '40s and early '50s, sports cars like Jaguar and MG had started selling consistently, though hardly in large numbers. Several American automakers decided that a home-grown sports car would do much better owing to customer loyalties and the easier parts and service availability domestic makes enjoy. Accordingly, there appeared the Nash-Healey, the Kaiser Darrin, and—most important in Ford's eyes—the Chevrolet Corvette. Dearborn replied with the 1955 Thunderbird.

In retrospect, the two-seat Thunderbird was a fluke, a good idea that didn't, in the end, sell in sufficient volume to satisfy the company accountants. Because of that, it was made into something entirely different: the post-1957 "Squarebird" with four seats. Interestingly, the transformation was underway even as the first two-seaters were being sold. Given the industry's normal three-year new-model lead time, it is easy to see that planning for a four-seater began no later than 1955. Though the two-seat Birds outsold Corvette, their volume was never enough to impress Ford management—particularly division general manager

Robert S. McNamara, perhaps the best-known of Henry Ford II's "Whiz Kids."

The Thunderbird project came together from two directions. Ford styling director Franklin Q. Hershey, ably assisted by young Bill Boyer, had been doing sports car renderings since 1950, hoping to interest management in putting such a car into production. Nothing much happened until Ford Division general manager Lewis D. Crusoe went to Paris for the 1951 automobile show. Strongly supported by his companion, George Walker—who was still an outside consultant working separately from Hershey—Crusoe felt

Early-1954 Thunderbird prototype

Late prototype for '55 Thunderbird

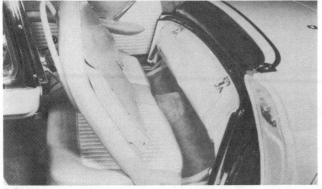
T-Bird top stowed behind seat.

1955 Thunderbird—smooth from any angle

1955 T-Bird's standard 292 V-8

'55 dash, telescopic steering wheel

a yen for a Ford answer to what he saw in Paris: the Spanish Pegaso, the revived Bugatti, the Jaguar XK-120, and the General Motors LeSabre show car. Crusoe reportedly asked Walker, "Why don't we have something like that?" "Oh, but we do," replied Walker—who then grabbed a phone to tell his people back home to get a sports car going. Both Walker's and Hershey's staffs started drawing up ideas for the sports-car-to-be. After GM introduced the Chevy Corvette in 1953, the project got going in earnest, which underlined Henry Ford II's determination to meet GM in every market sector.

The production Thunderbird was the work of Hershey and Boyer. The design was rapidly pushed through the usual stages of renderings, clay models, and steel prototypes, during which basic styling was gradually refined. Among ideas that went by the boards were Lincoln Futura-style taillights; a wide, eggcrate grille with a high-set bumper; numerous sheetmetal sculptures of the scoop-and-scallop school; fins and fangs of unmemorable proportions; and a bolt-on hardtop similar in appearance to the roof of the already-locked-up Continental Mark II. A sweepspear fender molding, similar (but not identical) to that of the 1955 Ford Fairlane, was shown in two early ads for the car, but was scrubbed before production began. The result was a timeless look that could hardly be improved upon. Meanwhile, there was the problem of what to call the thing. The eventual choice was one of about 300 candidates that included such monikers as Sportsman, Sportliner, Roadrunner, Runabout, Arcturus, Barracuda, Savile, El Tigre, and Coronado.

The first production Thunderbird came off the line on September 9th, 1954. The new model received gen-

Crusoe's personal '55 with "Fairlane stripes"

1956 Thunderbird

'56 porthole hardtop aided driver vision.

1956 T-Bird with soft top in place

1957 Thunderbird

1957 Thunderbird

erally favorable reviews. The only feature it shared with the Corvette was having two seats. A boulevard tourer rather than an all-out sports roadster, the Bird shunned snap-in side curtains for more convenient roll-up windows, fiberglass bodywork for traditional steel, and a six-cylinder engine for a potent V-8, a 292-cid Mercury engine derived from Ford's 1954 Y-block. With 193 horsepower, the T-Bird had plenty of zip to go with its good looks, and a respectable 16,155 of the 1955 models were sold.

An optional bolt-on hardtop was offered right from the start. Though it wasn't exactly the same shape as the Continental Mark II roof, it did have similar blind rear quarters that hindered over-the-shoulder visibility. A solution to this problem came for 1956 with the now-famous portholes. The ones used on a prototype hardtop were actually swiped from Bill Boyer's cabin

cruiser. Though the round shape didn't relate to anything else on the car, it somehow looked right. Buyers preferred the little windows to the blind quarters four-to-one. The '56 models also gained flip-out front vent panes to aid interior ventilation and —as a last-minute addition—an exterior spare tire mount. The latter was more a way to improve trunk space than a styling device, though it did come off well visually. The 292 engine was again offered for '56, but base horsepower was raised to 202. A new offering was a 312-cid V-8 with 215 bhp and somewhat more torque. The '56 model had a base price of $3151, against $2944 for the '55, and production leveled off slightly at 15,631.

Writer Karl Ludvigsen regarded the 1956 Thunderbird as a better balanced car than the '55, mainly due to a more equal front/rear weight distribution created by slinging the spare out back, "continental" style. Nevertheless, the roadability of early Birds was not genuinely sporting. The '55s used fairly stiff rear springs and quick steering. These were softened and slowed, respectively, for '56 because most buyers wanted it that way. As a result, the '56 (and 1957) Bird plowed a bit more on corners than the '55, and response to steering input in the 50-mph range was rather vague. The all-drum brakes were adequate for normal driving if not track work. The steering, though imprecise, was not completely robbed of road feel by excessive power assist. Today, the two-seaters still seem entirely up to date, and give away little in comfort or driving pleasure to cars several decades younger in the same weight and size class.

Despite its expected disadvantages as a competition car, the Thunderbird was raced—and did surprisingly well. In fact, it was far more capable than most people appreciated. At the 1955 Daytona Beach Speed Weeks, a T-Bird sponsored by Tom McCahill of *Mechanix Illustrated* magazine swept all honors among American production sports cars. Driven by Joe Ferguson, this car averaged 124.633 mph on a two-way run—better than any Austin-Healey, Porsche, and all but one Jaguar XK-120M.

The T-Bird did even better in 1956, when Ford hired ex-racing driver Pete DePaolo to prepare its cars. Chick Daigh drove a carefully set-up '56 to 88.779 mph in the standing mile, winning the production title in that class and very nearly besting a modified-class Corvette driven by Zora Arkus-Duntov (89.735 mph). But the Birds weren't entered in Daytona's long-distance race, and a Chrysler 300 won the Grand National that year. And the car wasn't competitive in road racing because of its soft suspension and indifferent brakes.

A serious facelift was mandated for the '57 Thunderbird. The front wore a bold combination bumper/grille, an idea Boyer had proposed for 1955 that was then considered too radical. The back end sprouted modest tailfins—a nod to Chrysler, but much less vulgar—flanking a longer rear deck. "We extended the trunk largely to get rid of the spare tire," Bill Boyer remembered. The 1957 Thunderbird was nevertheless four inches shorter than the '56 thanks to the spare's reabsorption into the trunk. (An optional exterior spare tire was listed for '57, and some models were so equipped.) Inside was a handsomely redesigned dash with a telescopically adjustable steering column (a feature on the '55). Door panel trim was modified, and featured a repeating Thunderbird logo.

The 1957 model was the most "styled" of the three-year two-seat generation. Still, Ford sales and product planning personnel resisted stylists' attempts to gook up the car with extra chrome, two-tone paint, and sheetmetal creases. They deserve a lot of credit, because what emerged looked good—and still looks good today. Production lasted longer than usual due to delayed release of the '58 Thunderbird, so the '57 set the two-seat sales record at 21,380 units.

Mechanical changes were small but significant. A new rear axle with straddle-mounted pinion gear was fitted, and fuel tank capacity was increased from 17 to 20 gallons. The strong frame and coil-spring front suspension were retained. Engineer Bill Burnett specified five-leaf rear springs (as in 1955) instead of six-leaf (as on the '56), and wheel diameter shrank from 15 to 14 inches. Engineers considered—and rejected—Edsel-style pushbutton automatic transmission controls. While transmission choices for '57 were the same as before, the engine range was greatly expanded—and now included a supercharged mill:

CID	Induction	CR	bhp	Trans*
292	2-bbl	9.1	212	b
312	4-bbl	9.7	245	ac
312**	4-bbl s'chgd	8.5	300	bc
312	2/4-bbl	9.7	270	abc
312	2/4-bbl	10.0	285	abc
312	4-bbl s'chgd	8.5	340	abc

*a = automatic   b = 3 speed   c = 3 speed overdrive
**only 15 built, for NASCAR homologation

The Paxton-McCulloch supercharger was supplied by McCulloch at the behest of DePaolo, who had learned that Chevrolet might offer a blower on the 1957 Corvette. A $500 option, this centrifugal unit delivered up to 6 psi of compressed air to a sealed carburetor. It did wonders for performance. Where the 245-bhp model would do 0–60 mph in 10 seconds and top out at 115 mph, the blown car would almost certainly see 125 mph maximum and run 0–60 in well under 7 seconds. A Ford-Q-Matic "F-Bird" driven by the editors was timed at 5.5 seconds in the 0–60 sprint (a time not corrected for speedometer error, which couldn't have been far off).

Only 208 supercharged Thunderbirds were built, and only another 1500 were fitted with the 270- and 285 bhp engines with eight-barrel carb. But Ford was not doing all this for fun; Daytona was again on management's mind. Accordingly, 15 blown cars with the 300-bhp setup were run off in order to homologate the package as "stock" in time for the 1957 Speed Weeks. There, Chuck Daigh scored 93.312 mph in the standing mile, and a privately entered Bird was clocked at 146.282 mph one-way, 138.775 mph both ways, in the flying mile. Unfortunately, the Automobile Manufacturers Association decided shortly after this to de-emphasize competition, and the T-Bird's racing career was nipped in the bud before DePaolo could develop the car further.

By this time, however, the Thunderbird had proven its merit. A sports car it wasn't—certainly not on a road course. A high-performance car it definitely was—at least the '57 could be with the right options. Had competition development continued, it showed every sign of becoming a serious super-stock contender in NASCAR. It is remarkable that this sort of performance was offered in a car so luxurious and lovely. It is an accomplishment in which, regardless of what happened in later years, Ford Division can take a great deal of pride.

Top: Wood-bodied Sportsman
convertible helped bring buyers back
to Ford showrooms. The 1947 model
is shown. Above: Wood trunk panels
required use of rear fenders and
taillights from the 1941 Sedan Delivery.

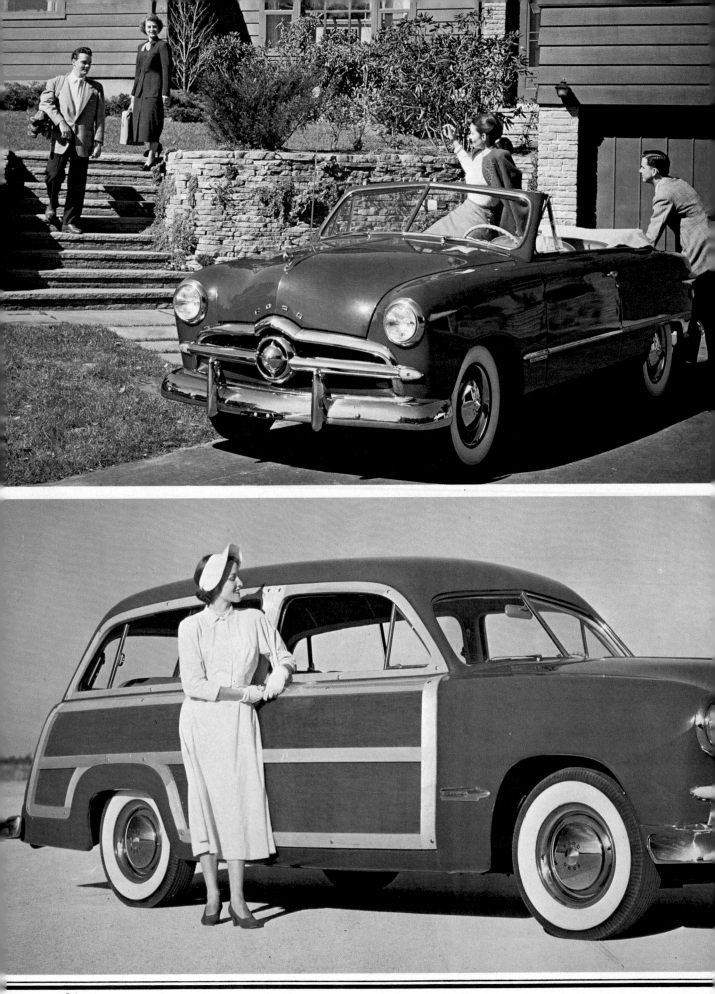

Opposite page: The all-new '49 Ford line featured clean looks and more up-to-date engineering. Among the more glamorous models were the rakish convertible (above) and the distinctive woodie wagon (below). Strong sales in 1949–51 were a major factor in Ford's postwar resurgence. This page, top: Eye-catching Crestliner two-door debuted for 1950 as a fill-in for a true hardtop, which arrived the following year. Two-tone paint, padded roof, and fender skirts were standard. Above: The 1954 Skyliner hardtop offered the industry's first see-through top, made of green-tinted Plexiglas. Excess interior heat buildup limited sales to some extent.

Above: Crown Victoria was available with and without a "bubbletop" for 1955 (shown) and '56. Rakish chrome roof band had no structural purpose, but looked nifty. Most "Crown Vickies" were fully equipped and had two-tone paint. Vee'd side trim was common to all models in the new '55 Fairlane series. Near right: A late prototype for the '55 Thunderbird. Note non-stock wheel covers and browless headlight rims. Far right, top and center: Thunderbird was an instant hit in 1955, easily outpacing its two-seat rival, Chevrolet's Corvette, in the sales race. Styling still looks good, and the model is highly prized in car-collector circles. Far right, bottom: A "continental" spare tire mount and portholes for the optional hardtop were the main appearance features of the '56 Thunderbird. A softer chassis gave a smoother ride at some expense in handling. New 312 V-8 was rated at 215 or 225 horsepower.

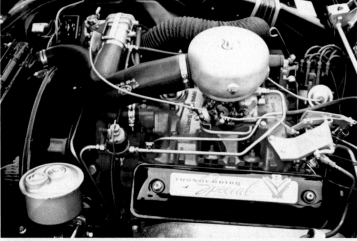

Above: The last of the two-seat Thunderbirds was handsomely facelifted with a large bumper/grille, modest blade fins, and elongated trunk. Left: The expanded 1957 T-Bird engine lineup included a twin four-barrel 312 (top) with 270 bhp, a supercharged 300-bhp version (upper and lower center), and a 245-bhp 312 with single four-barrel. Above right: The intriguing 1957 Skyliner retractable does its "disappearing act" in front of Ford's World Headquarters. Right: This view of the 1958 edition shows the Skyliner's shorter-than-stock roof and bulkier rear quarters. Model itself disappeared after 1959.

Above: Ford began working on a four-seat Thunderbird even as the first two-seaters were sold. It arrived for 1958 and proved immensely popular. The first Ford with unit construction, it opened up what would later be termed the "personal-luxury" market. Right and below: The first four-seater series continued through 1960 (shown) with mostly minor refinements. The big 430-cid Lincoln V-8 was made an option for '59 and a sunroof hardtop debuted for '60.

1957 Fairlane 500 Skyliner

1957-59 Skyliner
Somebody Had To Do It

There was *nothing* like the Ford Skyliner, the first —and only—retractable hardtop. To a gaping public in 1957, it was like something from Mars. Ford must have done a good deal of endurance testing on the complicated mechanism that made the car's top appear and disappear. If it didn't, it should have, because everywhere a "retrac" went, crowds were sure to go. Everyone wanted to see it "work." Ford advertising helped stimulate curiosity in this automotive side show by making a legitimate point: "How can it be a 'hardtop *convertible*' if the top doesn't go down?"

There's nothing new under the sun, and the retractable hardtop idea can be dated at least as far back as 1941. That's when Briggs Body Company stylist Alex Tremulis designed the Chrysler Thunderbolt show car, of which six were made. The Thunderbolt's top was relatively small, just large enough to cover the cockpit with its single bench seat, so the top could be easily withdrawn into the car's trunk. The 1957–59 Ford Skyliner (a name revived from "bubbletop" days) was a full-size, six-passenger car. At first glance, it did not look different from any other Ford. However, its rear fenders were longer by three inches and its top shorter by nearly four inches. From the rear, the Skyliner had a "bustle" look that clearly set it apart from its linemates.

The Ford stylist who suggested the retractable con-

cept was Gilbert Spear, whose designs convinced William Clay Ford to earmark $2.2 million for development. Bill, the younger brother of Henry II, was at that time the head of the Special Projects Division, which was working hard on a new Continental, the Mark II. The retrac was originally intended for that car until Special Projects decided to go with a conventional fixed top only in 1955. Ford Division then got the retrac project, but only after another $18 million had been invested for testing. The all-new 1957 Ford was only two years from introduction when the transfer was made, so a crash program had to be instituted for the Skyliner to be ready in time. Ford made it, introducing

1957 Skyliner prototype

the new car slightly later than the rest of the line in December 1956.

Most of the work, of course, went into the rear structure. There had to be room enough for that big roof and all the hardware needed to raise and lower it. The long rear decklid was hinged in the only possible way, at the rear. (The stylists just had to do what they could with the greater deck height, recontoured beltline, and blunt rear end that were unavoidable.) As mentioned, the greenhouse was shortened. The roof was given a hinge 10 inches from its leading edge, creating a flap that would fold under the top as it slid back. The new model was mounted on the Ford convertible chassis with the frame rails set closer together to create the outboard room necessary to accommodate the top's control linkage. Remarkably, rear seat legroom was not affected. Though about three inches of linear space were lost, engineers compensated by moving the Skyliner's rear seat further back than other '57 Fords. The gas tank took up valuable storage space in its standard location under the trunk floor, so it was put behind the rear seat, an "accidental" benefit to safety in a rear-end collision. The spare tire was placed in a small floor well.

The Skyliner's "nervous system" was composed of 600 feet of wiring running to no less than 10 power relays, eight circuit breakers, 10 limit switches, three drive motors, and a safety interlock that prevented anything from happening unless the transmission was in Neutral. If all that sounds complicated, it was—but when everything was working properly, the whole operation looked deceptively simple.

Here's how it worked. First, the driver would depress a switch (located on the steering column) with the ignition on (and preferably the engine running to minimize battery drain). This activated two (1957–58) or three (1959) switches to start the deck motor, which lifted the long lid via twin shafts mounted at each edge. As the deck locked into full-open position, it tripped the switch for another motor, mounted behind the rear seat, that raised the package shelf behind the seat to deck level. This in turn started another motor that unlocked the top. After this, two more motors (one on the 1959 model) started running to raise the top and send it rearward into the open trunk cavity. A separate servo folded the hinged front roof section as the roof eased its way back and down. A dashboard warning light, which glowed during the whole sequence, was then

1957 Fairlane 500 Skyliner

1957 Fairlane 500 Skyliner

Skyliner for 1958

extinguished, telling the driver to release the switch. This process could be reversed at any point. It was remarkably trouble-free considering the number of stages involved. In case of failure, the point at which the sequence stopped told a mechanic immediately where to look. A hand-cranked emergency manual override feature was provided so an unlucky owner wouldn't have to drive with the top stuck at half-mast.

The 1957 Skyliner was part of the new top-line Fairlane 500 series. Its price was $2942 or $437 more than the soft-top Sunliner convertible. For a car this specialized selling mainly on novelty value, it did respectably well. Ford built 20,766 units for the model year. It was just the thing to usher in the space age. This sales figure, as *Special-Interest Autos* magazine has pointed out, almost matched the two-seat Thunderbird's record year—and was more than twice the number of Corvette sales through 1960. Yet the retrac was *less* unique, and therefore involved less development expense, than either of those cars because it shared so much with the standard Ford line.

What it shared is worth noting. Ford dramatically restyled for 1957, achieving a rather blunt front face, but retaining smooth, flowing overall lines. The result was sleeker than the heavily facelifted '57 Chevrolet but not as eye-catching as the all-new Plymouth. Performance was a second language in Dearborn by now, and Ford offered a vast array of V-8s for '57. The Skyliner had the 190-bhp 272-cubic-inch powerplant standard, and Thunderbird engines of 292 (212 bhp) and 312 (245 bhp) cid were optional for all models. Fairlane and Fairlane 500 models rode a new 118-inch wheelbase, 2.5 inches greater than comparable 1956 cars (Customs and Custom 300s rode a 116-inch spread). The "longer, lower and wider" look plus new muscle meant strong sales in a prosperous year. Ford came within 130 cars of outselling Chevrolet, and by some calculations it was actually ahead. Whether or not it really was, the division enjoyed a moral victory with its '57 lineup.

A facelift for 1958 involved a Thunderbird-influenced bumper/grille combination, plus quad headlights and taillights and flashier side trim. Though this was exactly what the market seemed to want, 1958 was a recession year, and overall industry sales were well down. There were some mechanical improvements that make the '58 possibly the most desirable model in the Skyliner's three years. The big V-8 engines were fitted with larger valves and bearings plus a precision-molded, instead of forged, crankshaft. New three-speed Cruise-O-Matic transmission was introduced as an option for Fairlane and Fairlane 500, the first new Ford automatic since 1951. Finally, the Skyliner and all other Fords could be ordered with air suspension, with air bags, front/rear leveling valves, and a compressor-cum-tank in the engine compartment. Nevertheless, only 14,713 of the '58 Skyliners were produced. One reason for the sales decline was price: the base tag now read $3163, $513 more than a Sunliner convertible and $728 more than the fixed-roof Victoria two-door hardtop.

1958 Skyliner drops its top.

1958 Fairlane 500 Skyliner

For 1959, Chevrolet fielded its new line of radically styled "bat-fin" models that failed to catch the public fancy. Ford now passed Chevrolet with assurance, building about 12,000 more cars for the calendar year. Though heavily facelifted, the '59 Ford was recognizably of the same school as the 1957–58 styling. The Skyliner was now officially part of the new Galaxie series, which replaced the Fairlane 500 at the top of the line at mid-model year. So extensive was the '59 remake that the Skyliner itself had to be re-engineered. Base price rose to $3346, though most cars climbed over $4000 with options.

Ford had introduced its big 332/352 V-8s for 1958, available in 240-, 265-, or 300-bhp versions. They continued for 1959, but available horsepower was now 225/300 bhp. The company was beginning to tilt away from performance and toward fuel economy. The Skyliner still had a standard V-8, the 292-cid Thunderbird powerplant, which was an option on other models.

Despite the money that had been spent restyling the '59s, and re-engineering the Skyliner in particular, it was clear the retrac wasn't holding its own. Despite a record year for Ford Dvision, Skyliner sales dropped to 12,915, a three-year low. Accordingly, the model was dropped from the 1960 lineup after a total of 48,394 had been built. A reasonable number of these have survived, and there's a national club dedicated to preserving them. Skyliners of all years have also been named Milestones—outstanding cars built between 1945 and 1967—by The Milestone Car Society.

The Skyliner was done in by its high cost and inconvenience. The price premium over a conventional Sunliner, which had the same open-air appeal, grew each year; other models went up, too, but not as much. Also, the Sunliner had a commodius trunk even with its top down. The Skyliner, by contrast, had hardly any stowage space at all. To segregate baggage from the top and its retracting mechanism, Ford gave the car a small fitted luggage box measuring only 6.5 cubic feet. And you couldn't get to it with the top down *or* up except by manhandling it out from the side. The spare tire, stored underneath the box, was even harder to extract. Further, the Bob McNamara era at Ford meant the end of "gimmick engineering" and a shift to no-nonsense, high-volume sellers like the compact Falcon, which debuted for 1960. The big Fords became more conservative for a few years, then became interesting again in another way, with the advent of bucket seats, consoles, and high-performance engines.

It's probably just as well the Skyliner came and went when it did. There would be no place for it in the '60s, and Detroit was too busy with high-power V-8s and "hardtop convertibles" in the early '50s to spend the time or money necessary for such a device. But sooner or later somebody would have been moved to bring out a hardtop model that could convert itself into an open car, just as somebody saw a market for the hula-hoop, the two-tone ballpoint pen, and a refrigerator door you could open from two sides. Compared with inventions like these, maybe the Skyliner wasn't so strange after all— at least for the '50s.

1959 Fairlane 500 Skyliner

1958 Thunderbird Hardtop

1958~60 Thunderbird: Dynamite Times Two

*I*t's high time to correct misconceptions about the underrated 1958–60 "Squarebird," and to acknowledge this Ford as one of the greats. It was certainly among the outstanding American engineering achivments of the decade. Yet its success did not depend on technical gizmos like air suspension, fuel injection, supercharging or a retractable top. All of these were considered—and rejected—in designing the car that would be widely imitated as the epitome of "personal-luxury."

When Ford decided to make the Bird a four-seater it obviously decided against the two-seat concept. However, there were those in Dearborn who hoped both cars could be sold together as part of an expanded T-Bird family. Yet the decision that was made was sound. As a personal car, a four-seat Thunderbird made much more sense than a two-seater, and sales quickly proved it: 37,000 in the abbreviated 1958 model year, 67,000 for 1959, and a record 90,000 for 1960.

Thunderbird product planner Thomas Case had recommended retaining a two-seater for 1958 as "a marketing device to add some spiff to the program. It was not set up to be a profit program per se, although it turned out to be profitable." But Robert S. McNamara,

who had succeeded Lewis Crusoe as Ford Division general manager, wanted the '58 Bird to be a solid profit-maker, not just a glamor item. When he heard Case was angling to keep a two-seater in production he gave the young product planner what Case described as a chewing out: "Tom, it's dead. I don't ever want to hear of it again. I don't want anybody to do any more about it."

McNamara should not be viewed as a villian, because without him the Thunderbird might have died after 1957. Said stylist Bill Boyer, "McNamara really fought for it. He thought it was a good concept; he went in and fought for it [with the board of directors] and won." Part of McNamara's pitch was, of course, that a four-seater would make *real* money—which it did, by the bucketful.

The most innovative aspect of the '58 Thunderbird was its unit body—a fresh idea for Ford, but a concept that had been around in Europe since the 1922 Lancia and in Detroit since the 1934 Chrysler Airflow. Inspired by aircraft design practice, unit construction does away with a separate steel body attached to a frame with flexible mounts. Instead, it is a combined structure designed to be strong yet light, and able to absorb

Thunderbird for 1958 (left), '59 (center), and '60 (right).

1959 Thunderbird Hardtop

1960 Thunderbird Hardtop

1960 Thunderbird Convertible

stresses evenly. Also known as the monocoque principle, it tends to result in a tight, rattle-free automobile that weighs less than it would with traditional body-on-frame construction.

One problem with the "unibody" is its comparatively greater susceptibility to rust. Thunderbird body engineer Clare Kramer recalled the extensive measures Ford took to minimize the risk: "We developed a method of zinc-coating sheet steel heavily enough to meet our needs, with a minimum surface spangle that would not show through the final painted surface. This was used on the primary structures of the Thunderbird body. A paint drip process involving electrostatic adhesion of paint to the body was used in addition to the zinc coating of primary structure parts."

Unit construction was also ordained for the 1958 Lincoln and Continental Mark III, so Ford erected a new assembly plant at Wixom, Michigan to build these cars and the new Thunderbird. This made sense, because all were low-volume luxury models but accounted for enough volume between them to keep a plant busy. This also made unit construction economically feasible, since their lower volume would have made the cost of separate frames far higher than in the case of a high-volume car like the standard Ford.

Despite the fairly revolutionary nature of the '58 Thunderbird, Ford Division was alloted only $50 million for the whole project—$5 million for styling and body/chassis/engine engineering and $45 million for tooling. To economize on R&D, management decided to farm out body engineering to the Budd Company and the convertible prototype program to Wettlaufer Engineering. A few problems cropped up, but were solved in rapid-fire succession. "For instance," says body engineer Bob Hennessy, "we started in figuring the movement of the rear suspension [and found that] the car wasn't wide enough. We would be rubbing the sides of the wheel housing. . . . Since we were about two-thirds into engineering with die models in progress, we literally split the drawing down the centerline of the car and spread it apart.

"Inside the car there was really incredible room

when you consider we had reduced the overall height from the standard sedan by about 10 inches. This height had very much to do with the package drawing we engineers furnished Bill Boyer to style a vehicle around. . . . With a five-inch ground-to-floorpan height, 2½ to three inches for a seat track and electric seat motor, plus four inches of actual seat height, the driver's fanny was only 12 inches off the ground. This left us with a high tunnel on the inside, and, of course, the main integral frame sill section above the floor on the outside of the seat. The front seats were literally in a deep well." But Bill Boyer and his designers developed an ingenious dashboard extension that took advantage of this—one of the first uses of the central tunnel console in a modern production car.

Styling work began during 1955, with Boyer increasing the proposed wheelbase from 108 to 113 inches. A "formal" roofline with wide rear quarter pillars was adopted for its distinctive appearance and to keep decklid height down for the ultra-low stance the Sales Department was demanding.

Ford-Aire suspension had been planned for the 1958 Thunderbird, but was scratched because of its poor reliability record in other models. Instead, a complex coil-spring and trailing-arm rear suspension was used, the latter having been engineered especially for use with air bags. With Ford-Aire dead, conventional rear leaf springs were substituted for '59.

A 361-cid V-8 also bit the dust before the '58 was finalized. This engine, which was used in the larger Edsels, was to have been offered in four states of tune from 304 to 362 horsepower. But the Thunderbird project's tiny budget proved inadequate to cover the cost of the additional tooling necessary, so Ford Division settled for the 352 with 300 bhp. For 1959–60, the 430-cubic-inch Lincoln V-8 with 350 bhp was made an option.

The convertible body type was also in doubt until quite late in the game. It wasn't actually approved until May 1957, and didn't appear in dealer showrooms until June 1958. As a result, only 2134 convertibles were built for the 1958 model year. Once production hit its stride, however, soft-tops were turned out in decent numbers: 10,261 for 1959 and 11,860 for 1960. But this was only a small fraction of hardtop volume, which reached 57,195 units for 1959 and 76,447 for 1960. Also for '60, a third model with a gold-colored padded-vinyl top and special trim was offered at about $4000 base, and scored another 2536 sales.

The convertible's top mechanism was a complicated affair, similar in design to that of the Skyliner. The driver first unlocked the rear-hinged decklid by means of a remote-control button, then unhooked two windshield header clamps, manually raised the decklid, and lastly pushed another button to activate the folding mechanism. Late in the '59 model run the device became fully automatic via a single dashboard pushbutton.

The 1958 Thunderbird was such a success that Ford had to put Wixom on heavy overtime to keep up with demand, a refreshing change in a generally poor sales year. (The only other American make to gain that season was Rambler.) "We were making money so fast we didn't know what to do with it," said engineer John Hollowell. "It came, as I recollect, to somewhere around $1000 per car."

Under the circumstances there was little need to change the package. Aside from the switch to rear leaf springs, the '59 model was basically the same as the '58, though prices were up by about $50, to $3695 and $3979 for the hardtop and convertible, respectively. Apart from the newly optional 430 V-8, mechanical revisions were limited to a new auxiliary coolant tank and radiator fan and a relocated windshield washer system. Minor modifications were made to exterior tinware—a larger T-Bird emblem on the rear roof quarters, a new thin horizontal-bar grille pattern (repeated in the taillight appliqués), front fender ornaments with T-Bird insignia, pointed chrome on the door bullets instead of the previous hash marks, relocated Thunderbird script, and revised wheel covers. Inside, white replaced black on the instrument dials, and interior (as well as exterior) colors and combinations were shifted.

For 1960, Ford Division again elected to leave the package pretty much alone. One new option was a snug-fitting, sliding metal sunroof, the first among postwar American cars. Styling changes were confined to hash marks on rear fenders, cleaner side trim, a square mesh behind a large horizontal grille bar with three vertical dividers, three-element taillight clusters, standard outside rearview mirror, polarized day/night inside rearview mirror, revised interiors with built-in armrests, and a raft of new color combinations. Prices went to $3755 for the hardtop, $3967 for the sunroof hardtop, and $4222 for the convertible.

The four-seat Thunderbird was regarded as more luxury than performance car, but don't think it wasn't quick. With the 430-cid engine it would typically sprint from 0 to 60 mph in nine seconds flat, but used fuel at the drunkardly rate of 12 miles per gallon. Its main faults were a lack of nimbleness and, perhaps, practicality. In a test of the 1960 model, *Motor Trend* magazine noted: "Steering is slow and not precise. The driver's position limits visibility and makes control clumsy and restricted . . . [It has] some of the dimensional attributes of a compact and yet lacks some of those same characteristics of maneuverability associated with the type . . . [It is] nearly as costly as any standard luxury car, yet it has quality comparable only to a standard low-priced Ford . . . Its styling is distinctive but certainly not notable." These were curious comments considering the magazine had named Thunderbird "Car of the Year" for 1958.

But *MT* concluded on a sweeter note: "There were many cars that would outperform the four seater," it said. "But somehow the T-Bird has never been measured by these standards . . . It is a car apart, and like royalty, rarely required to count for ordinary deficiencies . . . These other qualities are, after all, quite commonplace. The Thunderbird is different, and that is all it has ever had to be."

1961 Thunderbird convertible and Falcon two-door sedan

1961-66 Thunderbird: Peak of Personal-Luxury

*T*he third- and fourth-generation Thunderbirds of the early '60s were the last of a type. Starting with the 1967 models the Bird became much larger. For a time, it was even available with four doors. For 1972, the T-Bird started sharing body and chassis with the Continental Mark IV. The next series was the down-sized 1977–79 derivative of the mid-size LTD II/Torino platform. The 1980–82 edition was simply a high-buck coupe based on the practical Fairmont compact. While the 1967–76 T-Birds still embodied the personal-luxury concept of the 1958–60 models, the later cars didn't—they were little more than gussied-up versions of a cheaper Ford product. Nevertheless, their introduction proved Ford still knew something about marketing in the late '70s. From a limited-edition car selling 50,000 to 60,000 units a year, Thunderbird became a mass-market model with sales topping 300,000 units for '77 alone. It still sells in similar quantities today.

However, for enthusiasts—people who love automobiles for their own sake—the "interesting" Birds stop after 1966. Historically, they were the best Thunderbird could offer in prestige and desirability. For many who bought a Corvair Monza or Falcon Futura

for their bucket seats, console, and sporty looks, a T-Bird was the ultimate personal car in the early '60s. And when or if they could afford it, these people would trade up to a Thunderbird. What they got was arguably the best Thunderbird of all. The 1961–66 models were cleverly engineered, nicely styled, and loaded with exclusive features offered by no other car. Ford coined a slogan that perfectly described the T-Bird in these years: "Unique in All the World."

Throughout its history the Thunderbird has generally kept to a three-year styling cycle. Thus it was that the 1961 model was to be all-new. Two clay mockups were in contention for '61 styling, one by long-standing Bird designer Bill Boyer, the other by Elwood Engel, both working under the then vice-president for styling, George Walker. Engel's angular, crisply lined proposal was eliminated when division general manager Robert McNamara decided it should be the basis for the "compact" 1961 Lincoln Continental, so Bill Boyer's work was once again the starting point for a new-generation Thunderbird.

Boyer remembered that his model "was very rocket-like in concept—very much aircraft-oriented, with big round 'flowerpot' taillights. It had what I called a 'fleet submarine bow.' We wanted to keep the thing very youthful, and of course that meant aircraft and missile-like shapes—a model as aerodynamically aesthetic as possible. In contrast, Elwood's was a very formal job, [thus] was perfectly suited to Lincoln." The two new cars, Boyer continued, had much in common: "Both featured very highly integrated bumper/grille combinations, for example. There was much similarity in the windshield and side glass, a lot of interchangeability."

From its sharply pointed front end, Boyer's design was tapered cleanly along the fuselage, with only the merest suggestion of a tailfin on the rear fenders. The 1958–60 "Squarebird" roofline was retained, but in a more rounded rendition. The original 1961 front end was a bit on the "chrome-y" side, and remained so through grille insert revisions for 1962 and '63.

Meanwhile, careful attention was being paid to interior design, guided by the talented hand of Art Querfeld, a 40-year Ford veteran. "I wanted to emphasize and delineate the positions of the driver and front seat passenger," Querfeld said. "I conceived of two individual compartments separated by a prominent console, which swept forward to the dash, curved left and right, meeting the doors and continuing around on the door panels." The console/divider was finished in brushed aluminum with horizontal lines. Querfeld said the modeling job was rough because of the complex curves involved. These "tended to warp or twist the banded aluminum if you weren't careful." One would never know it, looking at the final product, which was perfect.

Stuart Fry of the packaging team created the '61 Bird's unique "Swing-Away" steering wheel. This moved 10 inches laterally to the right (with the transmission in Park) to assist entry/exit. Pop-up roof panels were also considered, but rejected due to cost and complexity.

The third-generation Bird was not greatly changed in dimensions from the 1958–60 series. It retained a 113-inch wheelbase and 52.5-inch height, but was half an inch shorter and about an inch narrower overall. Body construction now followed the "dual unitized" principle, with separate front and rear sections welded together at the cowl. The cowl structure was shared with the '61 Continental, which helped keep tooling and production costs down and provided greater rigidity than in previous models.

Most engineering work for the '61 went into its completely redesigned chassis. There now appeared what engineers called "controlled wheel recession," which meant extensive use of rubber bushings to allow fore/aft as well as up/down wheel movement. This idea, then familiar Mercedes-Benz practice, marked another T-Bird "first" that would later be copied for many other U.S. cars.

The front suspension employed coil springs located above the upper wishbones. The lower control arm was a single bar instead of a wishbone, with a strut running from its outer end to a rubber bushing mounted on the unit body. At the rear, the forward spring mounts

1961 Thunderbird Hardtop

1961 Indy 500 Thunderbird Pace Car

were also carried in rubber bushings. Arms extended from the leaf shackles to each bushing to allow fore/aft movement. Stability was improved by increasing track width one inch at the front and three inches at the rear. Steering had a quicker ratio (20.3:1 instead of 25:1 as in 1960), which reduced turns lock-to-lock to 3.5 and allowed use of a smallish 16-inch-diameter steering wheel. The power-assisted, self-adjusting brakes had 14 percent more lining area than in 1960.

The sole T-Bird engine for '61 was a 300-bhp, 390-cubic-inch V-8, an enlarged version of the old 352. For 1962–63, Ford added an optional "M-series" 390, with three Holley two-barrel carburetors and 10.5 compression, which delivered a healthy 340 bhp. M-series Birds did 0–60 mph in 8.5 seconds, and had a top speed of 125 mph. The car reverted to the 300-bhp engine for 1964–65, but a big-block option was added for 1966.

The thoroughly overhauled chassis made the '61 T-Bird a much better handler than its predecessor. It took high-speed turns with little body lean, and would plow heavily only in tight corners. The quicker steering was more responsive, the enlarged brakes had better stopping power, and the "controlled wheel recession" made the '61 the smoothest-riding Thunderbird yet. Certainly it was the most comfortable American car on a wheelbase of less than 115 inches. And it was the best-engineered Thunderbird in history. Ford sold 73,051 units for 1961, of which 10,516 were convertibles.

Ever since the two-seat Bird had been discontinued, Ford management had constantly been receiving inquiries from dealers and customers who, though happy with the four-seater, wanted a little Bird, too. Product planner Tom Case even went so far as to propose a revival using the old dies—Tom never gave up! But it took Lido A. "Lee" Iacocca to bring back the two-seat concept after being appointed to succeed McNamara as division general manager (McNamara moved up to company president briefly, then joined the Kennedy Administration as Secretary of Defense). Though Iacocca could appreciate the two-seater's appeal, he didn't want to spend a lot of tooling money on one. His solution, thanks to some clever work by stylist Bud Kaufman, was the 1962–63 Sports Roadster.

Kaufman's idea was simple, though it took a lot of detail engineering to perfect. It was a fiberglass tonneau cover, with a pair of individual headrests for the front seats, designed to cover the rear seat area of the T-Bird convertible. Clever design allowed the top to be raised or lowered with the tonneau in place. Also, the tonneau didn't affect the front seats, which were still free to hinge forward so luggage could be stuffed in under the cover. But the tonneau was too big to carry in the trunk, so if you wanted to take extra passengers, you had to leave it at home. This, plus a tall price (about $5500 base) limited 1962 Sports Roadster sales to just 1427 units. And a mere 455 of the similar '63s were all that found customers.

Still, the Roadster was a dramatic-looking package. It was set off by standard Kelsey-Hayes wire wheel covers and skirtless rear wheel openings. Their spinner hubs made the wheel covers too bulky to fit under the normal T-Bird skirts (and they were too pretty to hide, anyway). Because of this rarity, the Sports Roadster has become the most desirable Thunderbird of the 1960s. The most exotic versions were equipped with the M-series engine, installed on only 120 of the '62s and 37 of the '63s.

Another new "package" model for 1962 was the Thunderbird Landau, a high-line hardtop distinguished externally by dummy landau bars on the roof quarters—another Boyer flashback to Classic-era styling. The Landau accounted for about a fourth of all Thunderbird hardtops built in this period. Its popularity stemmed not only from its unique looks but also a competitive price: at $4398 it cost only $77 more than the standard hardtop. Meanwhile, convertible production was slipping thanks to the increasing popularity of air conditioning. Ford built 7030 T-Bird ragtops for 1962, 5913 of the '63s, 9198 for 1964, 6846 of the '65s, and 5049 of the 1966 version. After that, the soft-top disappeared from the T-Bird lineup.

For the fourth-generation T-Bird of 1964–66, product planning took note of the competitive challenge from Buick's Riviera, launched for 1963. The Bird was accordingly given completely new sheetmetal featuring busy bodyside sculpturing, a bulging hood, and a dropped-center rear deck. Still keeping to a 113-inch wheelbase, designers put strong emphasis on quiet and refined luxury. The roofline retained the formal air of past models, but had a new feature in its "Silent-Flo" ventilation. By flicking a lever on the console, the driver could activate a servo that opened a full-width air vent under the rear window. The result was an extraction effect that pulled air entering at the cowl through the

1962 Thunderbird Sports Roadster

1962 Thunderbird Convertible

1963 Thunderbird Hardtop

1963 Thunderbird Sports Roadster

1964 Thunderbird Landau

car and out the vent into the slipstream behind. Flow-through ventilation had been seen as early as 1955 on the Mercedes-Benz 300 SL "gullwing" coupe and the stillborn Gaylord sports car. Mercury had introduced a retractable reverse-slant rear window on its 1957 Turnpike Cruiser, a feature Lincoln picked up for 1958. Though its purpose was the same it wasn't flow-through in the modern sense. So, Thunderbird can lay claim to another "first" among American cars.

Exterior styling of the 1964–66 series was overshadowed by a very jazzy interior, built around a dash that would have done justice to an airplane. No sport-

1964 Thunderbird Landau

1965 Thunderbird Convertible and Hardtop

1966 Thunderbird Hardtop

1966 Thunderbird Hardtop

ing driver liked the ornate speedometer with its red-banded drum pointer, or the chrome-trimmed minor gauges, or the plethora of highly styled buttons, knobs, and levers that sprouted from every corner. But Ford had the Mustang for the enthusiast crowd; Thunderbird owners simply loved their cars. Despite rivalry from the elegantly muscular Riviera, the T-Bird ran up satisfying sales totals. The '64 broke 1960's record with 92,465 units; the '65 sold 74,972 copies; and the '66 scored 69,176. No three-year generation did better. The 1964 figure was not exceeded until Ford adopted the mass-production LTD II bodyshell and cut the Thunderbird's price drastically for 1977.

Advertising said these Birds were "Begadgeted and Bedazzling," which was a fair description. Besides Silent-Flo ventilation, other new features included standard front disc brakes (1965), three-element tail-lights with sequential turn signals (1965), and a blind-quarter "Town" roofline for the Landau and hardtop (1966). Nor were these simply "luxurious bombs." A '65 Landau tested by *Car Life* magazine, for example, was said to be ideally suited for high-speed motoring: "So quiet and effortless was the running that the . . . speedometer too often crept well past the 80-mph mark . . . This is precisely the type of service for which the Thunderbird was designed—covering vast distances between two points in the shortest legal time with the least extraneous intrusions upon the passenger's serenity." *Car Life* ran 0–60 mph in 10.3 seconds, recorded a top speed of 115 mph, and scored 13 to 16 miles per gallon.

Road & Track magazine, which almost by definition favored the design attributes of small imported sedans and sports cars, was less sanguine about the Thunderbird than its then-sister publication. *R&T* said the '65 had "more symbolism than stature. Only the blessedly ignorant view it as anything more than what it is: a luxury-class car for those who want to present a dashing sort of image, who worry about spreading girth and stiffening arteries, and who couldn't care less about taste."

But it misrepresents *R&T* to quote that remark out of context. "Even when viewed in that light," the editors continued, "the Thunderbird must be admired. It is extremely well done for its purpose. Its roofline, its bucket seats, and console have inspired dozens of lesser imitations which, by their very imitation, proved the Bird a better beast. And certainly when viewed from outside, the body lines of the present version have an overall cohesiveness and sense of dynamism that few mass produced automobiles seem able to match."

Helped by such reviews, Ford just kept lining them up and shoving them out the door. Taking the performance critics to heart for 1966, it made the big-block 428-cid V-8 available as a Thunderbird option at just $64.30. This monumental powerplant and its 345 bhp shaved about 1.5 seconds off the Bird's 0–60 mph time, and extended its wings to the 120-mph region. Remarkably, it did not seem to have a big effect on gas mileage, which remained at around 10–15 mpg overall. And by introducing the big-block *after* the disc brakes, the engineers had kept their priorities straight: fast it might be, but the Bird would stop quickly, too—and in those days, not all big cars did.

For the collector, the Thunderbirds to look for among the 1964–66 models are the relatively low-production convertibles, the 45 or 50 Sports Roadster dealer conversions on '64 convertibles using leftover tonneaus and wire wheels from 1962–63, and the Limited Edition Special Landau of 1965 (4500 built). Together with the 1963–63 Sports Roadster, they stand to appreciate rapidly in value as these Birds become a more distant memory. One thing is certain: their memory will live on.

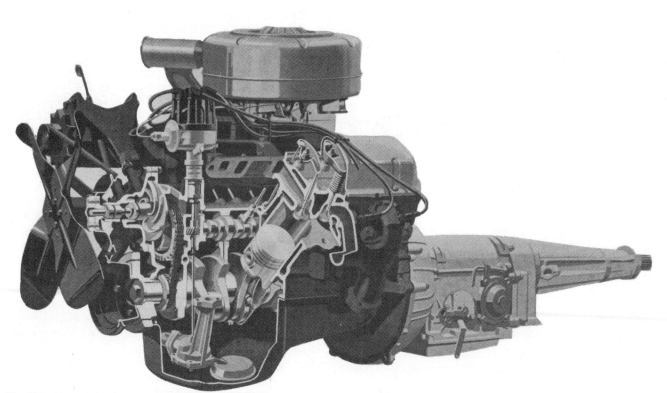

The 289-cid version of Ford's small-block V-8

Small-Block V-8s: Engineering Marvels

*W*hy did Ford decide to build a smaller V-8 in the early '60s? The answer is that, at that time, buyers started showing interest in more specialized models than Detroit had traditionally offered. As a result, the market soon split into several new size and price classes. As a "full-line" automaker, Ford competed in all of them, and actually started a few new ones. One of these was the "intermediate" class.

In 1960, Ford had decided to field a new series for '62 sized in between the compact Falcon and the full-size Galaxie. The Falcon was happy enough with a six, which originally displaced 144 cubic inches. The later 170-cid version was regarded as adequate for the base model in the new line, but the Fairlane, as it would be called, would also have to be offered with a more powerful engine as an extra-cost option. The Falcon six could not be enlarged beyond 200 cid, and it was the only modern six in the house. The 223-cid six used in the big Ford had been in production since 1952, and was due for replacement (which arrived for 1965 in a new, lighter 240-cid unit). A V-8 seemed the only logical answer, but there was a snag. Even Ford's smallest

"FE-series" engine, the 332-cid unit, was too heavy, too bulky, and too gas hungry.

So, a brand-new engine was clearly needed for the Fairlane. Displacement was pegged at between 220 and 230 cubic inches. Ford's engineering director, Harold C. McDonald, made a presentation to top management and got its approval for a completely new small-block V-8, a program representing an investment of some $250 million. Responsibility for design and development was handed over to a team led by George F. Stirrat. An Irish-born engineer who had joined Ford in 1949, Stirrat had spent his first years in Dearborn in a succession of assignments at Ford's Engine & Foundry operations. As a result, he was thoroughly familiar with every aspect of engine building from drawing board to manufacturing.

Stirrat's major objectives for the new V-8 were lightness and compact size. His targets were 20 inches maximum width and an installed weight of 450 pounds. He went to new extremes in order to make the block compact, selecting a 3.50-inch bore and a short stroke of 2.87 inches, plus short connecting rods and low piston height. He extended the block only as far as the crankshaft centerline instead of farther down into a deep, rigid crankcase. This layout did not even leave room inside the crankcase for full counterweighting— 30 percent of the engine's total unbalanced forces had to be handled by adding external masses. How and where? One balance weight was cast integrally with the flywheel. Another, located diametrically opposite it, was integrally cast with the crankshaft pulley adaptor at the front end. Bore centers were spaced at 4.38 inches, which allowed considerable freedom for later enlargement beyond the engine's initial 221 cid. On a compression ratio of 8.5:1, the new Fairlane V-8 delivered 145 bhp at 4400 rpm.

Stirrat's valvegear design was new to Ford, but was familiar Pontiac/Chevrolet practice. Rocker arms were mounted on ball-studs, thus eliminating rocker shafts. Valves were conventionally sized relative to bore, with head diameters of 1.59 inches for the intakes and 1.39 inches for the exhausts. Timing was fairly conservative, even for a volume-production V-8, at 21-51/57-15, giving an intake duration of 252 degrees and 36 degrees of valve overlap.

Despite weight-paring measures, Stirrat couldn't have met his 450-pound limit had it not been for newly developed foundry techniques. The man behind Ford's advances in thin-wall, high-precision casting was Harold C. Grant, who had joined Ford in 1932 as a machine operator and rose to become plant manager for the Dearborn Iron & Specialty Foundries. He was a leader in the development of nodular-iron castings and the shell-molding process using resin-filled cores. His work enabled Ford to keep out a lot of needless metal.

And more or less incidentally, the cast-iron Fairlane V-8 was a knockout blow for the aluminum-block engines then built in America: Buick's 215-cid V-8, and sixes from Chrysler and American Motors. The Buick and AMC engines were lighter, but Chrysler's 225-cid unit was heavier. All were far more expensive to produce. The Ford engine sent these rivals scurrying back to the iron foundries to copy its construction.

Fairlane V-8 production began in the fall of 1961. No sooner had it started than toolmakers were told to reset some of the machining lines for a 3.80-inch bore, which took displacement up to 260 cid. No changes were made to the cylinder head, but new pistons raised compression ratio to 8.7:1, and output climbed to 164 bhp. Back at the foundry, cores were also changed to maintain wall thicknesses and block strength. In the spring of 1962, Ford began offering the compact Falcon and Mercury Comet with a high-performance version of the 260. It was rated at 260 bhp—1 hp per cubic inch, one of the few engines in the industry to reach that magic figure in stock showroom tune. It served as the basis for the Ford V-8 that raced at Indy the following spring.

William H. Gay of Engine & Foundry took charge of the Indy program, and more or less blueprinted the cast-iron engine so aluminum could be used for block, crankcase, manifolds, and cylinder heads. The cast-iron crankshaft was replaced by one of forged steel,

260-cid size was short-lived.

and solid valve lifters replaced the hydraulic ones. Special rods were fitted, and bearing caps were reinforced to raise the rpm limit. It breathed through four double-throat Weber carburetors, and had electronic ignition and dry-sump lubrication. Power output was 375 bhp at 7000 rpm. Two Ford-powered Lotus cars finished second and seventh at the 500 that year.

At mid-model year 1963, Ford created a 289-cid version of the Fairlane engine by boring it out to 4.00 inches. This 289 became the base V-8 for the big Galaxie, and replaced both the 221 and 260 small-blocks for the 1965 Fairlane, Comet, and Mustang. The 289 had bigger valves. Head diameters on the base version were 1.67 inches and 1.39 inches for the intakes and exhausts, respectively. The Cobra version had even bigger valves and solid lifters. There was also a "Hi-Performance" 289 rated at 271 bhp at 6000 rpm. The Cobra came in at 380 bhp at 7000 rpm, and was chosen for the GT-40 sports/racing prototype with which Ford tried to beat Ferrari at Le Mans—and failed. Success came only with the Mark II car and its 427 Y-block engine. But there is a postscript to this: a GT-40 with a small-block 305 did win Le Mans in 1968.

This 305 was basically a race-tuned 302, which had been added for the 1968 model year as the standard V-8 for the LTD and as an option for the Mustang and Mercury Cougar ponycars. The displacement increase was obtained by giving the 289 a new crankshaft with a 3.00-inch stroke. Valve heads and cam profiles were changed slightly for the base versions. High-compression 302s rated at 230 and 250 bhp were also listed, with enlarged valves and, in the case of the latter, wild cam timing.

The 289 disappeared for 1969 and a 290-bhp "Boss 302" appeared after a few successful competition outings in 1968. The Boss, developed by William H. Gay, is significant, for it had new cylinder heads with the valves canted in two planes to give maximum cylinder filling at high rpm (an idea that stemmed from Chevrolet's "porcupine-head" 409 of 1964).

As a larger-displacement companion, Ford introduced the 351. This was basically a 302 redesigned by Phillip A. Martel, who had come to Ford from GM in 1950 to design a new family of tractor engines. He was also responsible for the design and development of the 429 and 460 V-8s (which replaced the FE-series). Now when you say 351, everybody thinks "Ah, the 'Cleveland' engine." But the Martel-designed unit is *not* the same thing. It is the "Windsor" engine, which went into production at the Canadian plant from which it gets its nickname in the fall of 1968, a full year before the Cleveland was introduced.

And the Cleveland was not a direct offshoot of the Fairlane family either, though it shared bore and stroke with the Windsor. It was the outcome of a separate program at Engine & Foundry by Frank J. Miller and J. J. Van Duen. That in turn led to Ford's 400-cid V-8, introduced as an option for the 1971 Galaxie and LTD, and which had nothing in common with the bigger 429 and 460 V-8s apart from the number of holes in the block.

Both 351 engines had a 4.00-inch bore and a 3.50-inch stroke. The Windsor featured increased bulkhead strength in the block, a deck height raised 1.27 inches, and a new crankshaft with larger main and crankpin journals. Its intake manifold was of drop-center design, and its valvetrain included "positive-stop" rocker arm studs. The bore spacing of 4.38 inches, as in the original Fairlane 221 V-8, was also retained for the Cleveland engine. When it came into production, the Windsor unit was relegated to a secondary role, used mainly in base form with low compression and two-barrel carburetion. The Cleveland engine became the basis for nearly all the high-performance Fords from 1970 through the end of 1974.

Ford spent some $100 million on tooling for the Cleveland engine. Its block casting was different than the Windsor's, with an integral timing chain chamber and water crossover passage at the front end. Its deck height was increased exactly 1.00 inch above that of the 302 block. Cylinder heads were dramatically different from the Windsor's, being directly derived from the Boss 302 design. Valves were canted 9.5 degrees from the cylinder axis to give a modified wedge-type combustion chamber. In addition, the intake valves were tilted 4 degrees, 15 minutes forward and the exhaust valves 3 degrees backward to give shorter port areas with more direct gas flow. The valves were placed as far apart as possible so they could be as large as possible. Intakes had a 2.19-inch head diameter, and the forged-steel exhaust valves were 1.71 inches across their aluminized heads.

The Cleveland V-8's valvegear was also new in several important details. Independently mounted rocker arms had wide cylindrical fulcrums in place of the usual ball-stud mounts. These fulcrums seated in guide slots milled into the mounting pedestals of the cylinder heads to give more positive control over rocker arm movements. Valvetrain durability was enhanced by shorter, stronger pushrods; a new camshaft; and stiffer valve springs (with inner dampers on four-barrel engines).

A Boss edition of the Cleveland engine followed for the 1971 Mustang, with power increased from 300 to 330 bhp (SAE gross) at 5400 rpm on an 11.0:1 com-

pression ratio. Its installation weight was 584 pounds, giving the car a remarkably high power-to-weight ratio, even in comparison with the hot 289s. A few months later came the 351 CJ (Cobra Jet) with an output of 280 bhp (SAE net). It differed in being able to run on regular-grade gasoline despite its 9.0:1 compression. It had a new high-lift camshaft, but used hydraulic rather than mechanical lifters. After two years of production it fell victim to the fuel crisis.

After the 1974 model run, the Cleveland engine was revised, its code designation changing from 351-C to 351-M (Modified). Eventually, it too would be doomed by the demand for greater fuel economy that spelled the end of large-displacement V-8s.

The Cleveland engine plant then concentrated on building the 302 and, since 1980, a 255-cid derivative. This was created by reducing bore to 3.68 inches while retaining the 302's crankshaft and 3.0-inch stroke. A lot of work went into lightening this powerplant, and it weighed some 60 pounds less. The 255 delivered 115 bhp with two-barrel carburetor or 120 bhp in four-barrel form. It saw wide corporate duty for 1980.

The 351 Windsor unit survived through the 1981 model year in two forms, 145 and 185 bhp, after which it was withdrawn for commercial sale (though it was still available for police vehicles). The 302 was modified with electronic fuel injection for 1980 to power the big Lincoln Continental (later Town Car) and Continental Mark VI. And in carbureted form it was pressed into service for the 1982 "baby" Lincoln, the bustleback Continental sedan.

Perhaps the most welcome news for performance fans was the return of the 302, in modified form, as the top power option for the 1982 Mustang/Capri. Special features included a larger-flow (356-cfm versus the normal 310-cfm) two-barrel carb, a larger 2.5-inch-diameter "streamlined" exhaust system, and a low-restriction air cleaner with twin snorkels. A special camshaft with wilder timing, originally developed for a marine version of the 302, was also fitted. These changes boosted power output to a rated 155 bhp (SAE net) at 3400 rpm, with 235 lbs/ft peak torque developed at a lazy 1800 rpm. Significantly, this latter-day "muscle" engine was offered only with four-speed manual transmission, and could quite easily shoot a Mustang/Capri to the magic 60-mph mark in under 8 seconds.

The story of Ford's tough, torquey small-block V-8 is far from finished. It won't last forever, of course, because of the continuing demand for improved fleet-average fuel economy faced by all Detroit automakers. But it does show every sign of outlasting the famed flathead V-8's long 21-year production run despite the enormous changes in engine design that have had to be made to meet government economy and emissions regulations. That fact alone is enough to make it a marvel of adaptability, not to mention staying power.

So, after a decade of dullness, performance is making a comeback in Dearborn. If you don't believe it, a short hop in a 302-equipped '82 Mustang or Capri is bound to change your mind.

1963 Falcon Futura Sprint Hardtop

1963~65 Falcon Sprint: Petite Sport

Elsewhere in these pages we detail the masterful engineering of the thin-wall Fairlane 221/260/289 V-8 and precisely why it was one of the milestone engines of the postwar years. Thanks to its compact size and high-performance capabilities, it found its way into a lot of exotic machinery during the '60s—the A.C.

Genesis of the Sprint: 1960 Falcon

Cobras, Shelby-Mustangs, and Sunbeam Tigers among the more notable. The Mustang and its overwhelming popularity tended to overshadow one of the best small-block cars of the decade, the winsome Falcon Sprint. It still does. The Sprint remains a relatively unknown quantity in car-collector circles, while the number of people buying early Mustangs these days is huge.

Were it not for the Mustang, the Sprint might have been developed into a truly international, rally-bred, highly competitive, and satisfying sports compact along the lines of the British Ford Cortina-Lotus. But its sales were only a tiny fraction of the Ford ponycar's:

Year	Hardtop	Convertible
1963	10,479	4,602
1964	13,830	4,278
1965	2,806	300

For 1966 the Falcon was redesigned for the third time in five years. The Sprint was dropped, and has since been almost forgotten. But not by us.

Origins of the Sprint are directly traceable to the success of the Corvair Monza. The standard, de-trimmed, underpowered Corvairs proved a disappointment for General Motors. They were heavily outsold by the more conventional Falcon, and Chevrolet quickly fielded the Chevy II for 1962 to fill the gap. But along the way something entirely unexpected happened. When Chevy introduced a luxuriously trimmed, bucket-seat Corvair coupe called the Monza in early 1960, it sold like nickel beer on a hot August day. When a four-speed gearbox was offered for 1961, it sold even faster. And when a Monza convertible arrived in 1962, the buying public went wild.

At this time, Ford was still following Henry Ford II's dictum of meeting GM wherever and whenever it could. So, the Falcon Futura was duly announced for mid-1961 to answer the Monza challenge. The Futura offered the same sort of mildly posh, bucket-seat interior (complete with Thunderbird-style console/glovebox) as the Monza. It was fairly successful, accounting for about 45,000 sales in its first model year, though that was still about 90,000 less than the Monza's total. So, Ford decided to expand the series for 1963 with a four-door sedan, two-door hardtop, and convertible. Together with the original two-door sedan, they notched well over 100,000 sales. The only trouble was that the Futura came only with the reliable, but anemic, six-cylinder Falcon engines. The Fairlane V-8 was hardly in production when Ford engineers decided to stuff it into the Falcon. The result was dubbed "Sprint," and it couldn't have been a more timely idea.

The 164-bhp, 260-cid small-block made the humdrum Falcon into an honest performance machine. *Car Life* magazine, which called the Sprint "Le Petite Sport," noted that it reduced the normal Falcon's power-to-weight ratio from 31.4 lbs/bhp to 21.0. The 260, *CL* said, was "a willing engine. If it seems unaware of the choking restrictions of its single 2-barrel carburetor, it is because of somewhat generous valve sizes and relatively clean intake and exhaust designs. Its ability to readily surpass the 5000-rpm redline would have one believe it is fitted with mechanical lifters, but, of course, it isn't. The engine is completely devoid of fussiness, and exhibits a surprising amount of torque from rather ridiculous rpm levels. Despite the ease of over-revving, there is a decided leveling off of output at the power peak, so that raising the shift points makes no improvement in acceleration. This engine is much happier in the Falcon surroundings than it ever seemed to be in the Fairlane, particularly when it had been teamed (in the latter car) with the 2-speed automatic transmission." *Car Life* recorded 0–60 mph in 12 seconds, the quarter-mile in 18 seconds at 75 mph, and a top speed of 105 mph for its four-speed '64 Sprint.

Part and parcel of the Sprint package was its new slopeback roofline, which gave better streamlining—not to mention a prettier profile—compared to workaday Falcons. For 1965, the 260 was superseded by the 289 V-8. With horsepower options all the way up to 271 bhp, it made the Sprint even more of a stormer. The highest base price ever asked for these fine little

1962 Falcon Futura Two-Door Sedan

1962 Falcon Futura Sport Coupe

grand tourers was $2671 for the '65 convertible, making this one of the great bargains of the '60s.

As one of "The Lively Ones" introduced for 1963½, the Sprint signalled a new, across-the-board emphasis on competition at Dearborn, and Ford Division in particular. Everywhere there was a race—NASCAR, USAC, the drag strips, European rallies, the sports-car circuit—there would soon be a Ford or Ford-powered car contending for honors. The Shelby Cobras and Ford GT-40s were tangible evidence of this corporate enthusiasm, and everyone who loves cars can thank Ford for helping to make those years a time of unbridled excitement.

Ford decided to showcase the Falcon Sprint by attacking the rough-and-tumble European rally circuit—something never before attempted with an American car. Rallying "across the pond" is far different from the time-speed-distance computer-matches held in North America. Cars are run over long-distance legs on regular roads, most of them narrow, challenging, and, in winter, downright treacherous. And the Sprint's rally debut was to be in the toughest rally of all, the gruelling Monte Carlo. Three rather special Falcon Sprints were entered in the over-3.0-liter "Standard or Modified Production" category. Their engines were tuned to the same level as Carroll Shelby's concurrent Cobras: 260 horsepower (one bhp per cubic inch). The driving teams were Anne Hall and Margaret McKenzie; Trant Jarman (Detroit) and Peter Jopp (England); and Bo Ljungfeldt and Gunnar Haagbom (both Swedes, the latter having been Eric Carlsson's partner and co-winner of the 1962 Monte Carlo).

Jarman later spoke of his experience, recalling the frightful weather faced by the Ford team: "All three of us started from Monaco, which was pretty easy. From

Gap to Bollene the snow and ice began getting a little worse . . . We were making it all right, but things were happening. First we ran into a cat stuffing snow down his radiator in the middle of the road . . . Then as we progressed a little further, we stopped a minute to pull Anne and Margaret [Hall/McKenzie] out of the snow. We weren't on spikes [tires] at the time, but as we continued we met Bo, who was putting on spikes . . . so we did too."

Jarman and Jopp carried on through the arctic landscape, occasionally passing other cars stuck in the snow, caught nose down in colossal drifts or simply buried in the muck. At the end of the first leg in Rennes, France, they and the Ljungfeldt/Haagbom Sprint were among 15 survivors of the 32 cars that had started from Monte Carlo. The ladies had lost much time, and had been penalized beyond recovery, but the other two Falcons were running 1–2 in their class.

Although the much faster "Grand Touring" class cars dominated the final standings, Ford managed to astound the Europeans. Against the overall winner's 2992 penalty points (Carlsson's Saab), Jopp/Jarman had been penalized only 3657 points, Ljungfeldt and Haagbom 3898.

The Sprints did best in the "special stages," which tested the cars over timed sections including the formidable Mount Ventoux hillclimb. Said Jarman: "The success that the Fords had is indicated by Bo Ljungfeldt, who established the fastest time on every special stage of the six, from Chambery down to the finish at Monaco. I don't think that this has been achieved before in the history of the Monaco rally—one man the fastest of all on every special stage. I think the explanation is the Swedish spikes, which have about 600 spikes per tire, approximately half-inch tungsten tips. [With them] the cornering ability is fantastic. You can go in very late, start a slide, and use a dirt-track technique where you're pointing the car with the throttle at all times. Ljungfeldt doing this is a tremendous sight.

"I got to like our Ford tremendously. I thought we were sitting in the best equipment that was there. The cars that I *respected* were the ones that did well. The Saab, Citroén and the Cooper-Mini impressed me . . . [The Falcons] were tremendously well prepared. Peter and I, for instance, had absolutely no mechanical problems throughout the entire rally, just brake pad wear. The transmission, the engine—even with the revs we were using—were without any servicing at all at the finish. I believe we could have gone around again. The cars were magnificent."

The final test of the rally was three laps of the famed Monaco Grand Prix circuit, laid out over the city streets of Monte Carlo, a total distance of about six miles. Here, the Falcon Sprints were awesome. Against a time of 6 minutes 1.8 seconds (by a 2.0-liter GT Porsche), Ljungfeldt recorded 6:22.3 in his Falcon, and Peter Jopp 6:32.4. The only cars ahead of Ljungfeldt were the Porsche, an Austin-Healey and a Triumph TR-4—the latter by a mere tenth of a second.

Though it lasted through the '63 Monte, the Sprint itself didn't last long on the market. Though the re-

1964 Falcon Futura Sprint Convertible

1964 Falcon Futura Sprint Hardtop

Sprint Cousin: 1965 Falcon Futura Convertible

designed Falcons of 1966 were offered with performance engines up to and including the burly 390, they were larger and more unwieldly, and thus not very suitable for international rallying. Anything larger than the 1963–65 Sprint was just too big. "There are places on the route that you couldn't get a few of the really large cars through," Jarman noted. "Ford was accused of moving villages around a little. I don't think the [Sprint] was too big, but I think it is about at the limit."

Today, you can find Falcon Sprints in good condition for under $3000—and occasionally for under $2000, which is food for thought. If you're looking for a compact-sized collector car with practical four-passenger capacity and a thoroughbred's heritage, you might want to pick one up. Then you could pretend you're Bo Ljungfeldt. You may not quite be able to duplicate one of his sideways slides down Mount Ventoux, but you will have the satisfaction of driving a retired champion, without a doubt one of the great cars from Ford.

1965 Mustang Hardtop (prototype)

1965~68 Mustang: The Ford That Couldn't Miss

$\mathscr{F}$ord wishes it had a car like the 1965 Mustang today. When it was introduced on April 17, 1964 as a 1965 model, the Mustang made more news than Barry Goldwater sewing up the Republican Presidential nomination. America went wild over this sporty, long-hooded Ford—the first in a long line of automobiles that would become known, in its honor, as "ponycars." Ford had projected first-year sales of 100,000 units. The final model year total (through December 1965) was an astounding 680,989. A legend had been created overnight. And the legend's base price was only $2368 f.o.b. Detroit.

The Mustang was born during 1961 meetings of the Fairlane Group, an informal eight-man executive committee headed by Lee Iacocca that met regularly at the Fairlane Inn in Dearborn. The group's assignment was to come up with a new, youth-oriented car to capitalize on growing buyer interest in bucket-seat compacts with four-on-the-floor. The group considered and decided against both a revival of the 1955–57 Thunderbird (the "XT-Bird") and a production model patterned after the experimental Mustang I, a lightweight, mid-engine design with all-independent suspension and Triumph/MG proportions. The reason in both cases: only two seats. Iacocca's team shrewdly realized that such a car would have limited appeal—and none for young couples with children, or indeed anybody who occasionally needed back seat carrying capacity. The decision was made to go with the "median sports car," a four-seat proposal that established size and packaging requirements for the new model. Now, all Styling had to do was to develop an appropriate character for it.

During late 1961 and throughout 1962, Ford stylists produced scores of proposals. The one that ultimately impressed Iacocca most was a white-painted clay model dubbed Cougar. This low, sleek hardtop came from the Ford Division studio under Joe Oros, Gail Halderman, and David Ash, one of several teams competing in what amounted to a not-so-friendly intramural design contest. A running prototype styled around this car called Mustang II was constructed, and very closely resembled the production car-to-be. It was shown to the crowd at the United States Grand Prix in the autumn of 1963. By then, of course, the production model had been nearly locked up in all aspects. All indications were that it would meet Iacocca's goals: 2500 pounds curb weight, a base price not more than a dollar a pound, and looks that said "young."

The Mustang was mainly a body engineering project. This was because, again at Iacocca's direction, the chassis, engine, suspension, and drivetrains would all be off-the-shelf Falcon and Fairlane bits, an essential part of the plan to keep the new car affordable. At 181.6 inches, the Mustang had the same overall length as the 1964 Falcon, though wheelbase was slightly shorter. Both hardtop and convertible body styles were planned, and Ford engineers projected the use of both the Falcon six-cylinder engine as well as the efficient 260-cid Fairlane V-8. The 170-cid six would be standard, along with three-speed manual gearbox with floorshift, full wheel covers, padded dash, bucket seats, full carpeting, and a color-keyed interior.

A key part of the Mustang concept was a veritable smorgasbord of optional equipment so each customer would be able to personalize his or her particular car. The menu included self-shift Cruise-O-Matic, four-speed manual, and three-speed-with-overdrive transmissions; a choice of three different V-8s; limited-slip differential; "Rally-Pac" (tachometer-and-clock combo wrapped in a small pod around the steering column); handling package; power and front disc (late 1965) brakes; power steering; air conditioning (except with the Hi-Performance 271-bhp V-8); center console; deluxe steering wheel; vinyl roof covering; pushbutton radio; knock-off style wheel covers; 14-inch styled steel wheels; and whitewall tires. There were also option *packages:* a Visibility Group (mirrors and windshield washers); an Accent Group (striping and rocker panel moldings); an Instrument Group (needle gauges and round speedometer); and a GT group (disc brakes, driving lights, and special trim). The most expensive extra was air conditioning at $283. Many desirable accessories were bargain priced: handling package ($31), disc brakes ($58), Instrument Group and Rally-Pac ($180).

While six-cylinder Mustangs sold reasonably well, most buyers ordered one of the wide range of V-8s. The smallest was the 260-cid unit with 164 bhp. Derived from this, and later replacing it, was a 289 offering 195/200 bhp with two-barrel carburetor or

Mustang I experimental, 1962

Mustang I experimental, 1962

Mustang II show car, late 1963

210/225 bhp with four-barrel. Finally there was the "Hi-Po" 271-bhp 289. The normal four-barrel 289 cost $162 extra, and the tuned version was $442. (For more details on these fine V-8s see Chapter 12.)

Though the car was certainly attractive, it was not exotic or earth-shaking in appearance. But it looked light, agile, and clean, and suffered only by a few lapses. The most criticized were the non-functional bodyside "scoops" ahead of the rear wheel openings and the shallow, high-set grille that looked a bit awkward. Space utilization, given a fairly ample wheelbase, was poor, leaving the rear seat only marginally habitable by adults. Sports car magazines took issue with the driving position, the sloppy standard suspension, and the "borrowed" (from the Falcon) dash.

Properly optioned, however, the Mustang was a horse of an altogether different color. A 271-bhp model tested by *Road & Track* magazine returned blazing acceleration (0–60 mph in 8.5 seconds, the standing-start quarter-mile in 15.6 seconds at 85 mph, and a top speed of 120 mph). Its optional handling package (larger front anti-roll bar, 5.90 × 15 Firestone Super

1965 Mustang Convertible

1965 Mustang Convertible

1965 Mustang GT 2+2 Fastback

1965 Mustang GT 2+2 Fastback

1966 Mustang Hardtop

Sports tires, quick steering ratio) "eliminated the wallow we experienced with previous Mustangs [and tied] the car to the road much more firmly, so on a fast run the point of one's departure into the boondocks is delayed very considerably . . . There is a certain harshness to the ride at low speeds over poor surfaces, but this is a small price to pay for the great improvement in handling and roadholding." The editors called the Mustang 271 "a big step in the right direction."

Road & Track was the harshest of the reviewers. Most other publications liked the car about as much as the buying public. *Motor Trend* magazine's 271 did 0–60 mph in 7.6 seconds, and ran the quarter-mile slightly faster than *R&T*'s car. It was obvious that with the right equipment, a Mustang could be a very interesting and satisfying automobile.

At the start of the official 1965 model year in the fall of 1964 a third body style was added to the Mustang stable, a nimble-looking fastback. Priced about $200

above the hardtop and mere pocket change below the convertible, it was a sales winner. Over 77,000 were sold for the model year, against 102,000 covertibles and—the really stupendous figure—over half a million hardtops.

With sales like that Ford wasn't about to tamper, so the 1966 Mustang was almost a carbon copy of the orginal. Up front, the single horizontal grille bar was replaced by several thin bars as backdrop for the galloping horse emblem. The fuel filler cap was modified, but nothing else changed at the rear. Along the bodysides, the simulated scoops were decorated with windsplits, nameplates were mildly revised, and wheel covers were restyled. Inside, the "bargain-basement" standard gauge cluster with strip speedometer was replaced by the more comprehensive five-dial instrumentation previously listed as an option. The Rally-Pac remained an extra-cost item. Engines were reduced to four. The base unit was now a 200-cid ohv six (the 170 was dropped). Optional were three 289

1966 Mustang GT 2+2 Fastback

1966 Mustang Convertible

1967 Mustang Hardtop

1967 Mustang GT Fastback

1967 Mustang GT Fastback

V-8s offering 200, 225, and 271 bhp. The option list was extended to include a stereo tape system and deluxe seatbelts with reminder light.

Overall sales of the '66s were not as high, because the '65 model year was longer than normal owing to the Mustang's early introduction. But for comparable 12-month periods, the '66 actually did better—by 50,000 units. Of course, Mustang still had no direct competitors. Chevy was a year away from launching its new Camaro, and sales of its Corvair were dwindling. Plymouth's hastily created Barracuda was recognizably just a fancy Valiant with a glassy fastback roof, and its sales were way behind Mustang's. So, Ford happily counted the proceeds from selling a model year total of 35,000 fastbacks, 70,000 convertibles, and nearly a half million hardtops.

With the Camaro and Pontiac's Firebird in the running for 1967 and the Barracuda nicely redesigned, Mustang faced tougher sledding. But Dearborn knew something of its competitors' plans in advance, and

had readied some new features for the '67 Mustang. Chief among these was a bold engine option, the broad-shouldered 390-cid Thunderbird V-8 with four-barrel carburetor and 320 bhp. With the six and the returning trio of 289 V-8s, this extended the total number of available powerteams to 13.

The 390 made the Mustang very brawny, but unfortunately it also brought a heavy front-end weight bias. Agile handling was not this model's forte despite its standard F70-14 Firestone Wide Oval tires. The optional competition handling package (stiff springs, thick front anti-sway bar, Koni shocks, limited-slip differential, quick steering, and 15-inch wheels) was almost mandatory with the big-inch mill. It was also available with the 271-bhp 289, making a Mustang so equipped a grand tourer in the international idiom. But if you wanted to run seven-second 0–60 mph wind sprints and 15-second quarters, the 390 was the only way to go. Drag racers loved it.

Ford improved the 1967 Mustang in several ways.

Sheetmetal was revised from the beltline down on all models for a beefier look. Fastbacks gained a sweeping new roofline to replace the semi-notch effect used for 1965–66. Other appearance changes were a concave tail panel and a few extra inches in the nose to go along with a more aggressive grille. Engineers pitched in with new rubber bushings at suspension attachment points for reduced noise and vibration and a wider track for improved handling response. A general front suspension rework decreased the car's understeering tendency without the stiff springing that previous models had needed for good handling.

It was almost a foregone conclusion that Mustang sales would decline in the face of competition, and indeed they did—by about 25 percent. Most of the loss was sustained by the hardtop, but convertibles also suffered, trailing fastbacks for the first time. Yet the 1967 model year total of 474,121 units led the ponycar field by a wide margin. Interestingly, that was still better than *double* the most optimistic estimates of Ford's marketing mavens for the Mustang's *first* year.

The decline continued. Sales of the '68s were down considerably despite a generally improved year for the industry as a whole, including Ford Division. The problem was that the field where only Mustang had stood two years before was now occupied by a herd of ponycars. GM and Chrysler models were out in force, and American Motors had its attractive new Javelin. Mustang prices had also gone up. The '68 convertible, for instance, started at around $2800, but could easily exceed $4000 with a few options. There was even competition from within Ford Motor Company itself—direct in the form of the Mercury Cougar, and indirect in the form of the Torino and Mercury Cyclone.

Another problem was that Mustang wasn't changed much for '68. It was still obviously the same car that had wowed the public in 1965, but by now it was a familiar face. The '68s were offered with the usual broad choice of engines, though some had been detuned to meet new federal emissions standards. Emission considerations led to development of a new 302-cid "mid-performance" V-8, a stroked version of the 289, delivering 230 bhp. Like its small-block forerunners, it was tractable, efficient, and reasonably economical. It added about $200 to the bottom line.

Another new optional engine for '68, priced at a formidable $755, was the Ford 427, a semi-hemi powerhouse with 10.9:1 compression and packing a 390-bhp wallop. Its steep price and its heaviness (which tended to overload the front suspension) kept it from being very popular. It was sold only with Cruise-O-Matic transmission, though it would have been something else with a four-speed and a stump-pulling axle ratio. The 427 car's typical 0–60 mph times were in the neighborhood of six seconds, the fastest yet for a showroom-stock Mustang in a straight line.

At over 300,000 units, 1968 Mustang sales were not something to celebrate, at least compared to previous seasons. But the pace set in the first three model years was so torrid that it would have been hard to sustain by any means. So in a sense, 1968 was a "stopgap" year, during which Ford Division was satisfied to stand pat. There was a very good reason for this: it was brewing some surprises for 1969.

1968 Mustang Convertible

1968 Mustang GT Fastback

1968 Mustang CS (California Special) Hardtop

CS was originally GT/SC (Sport Coupe)

1970 Mustang Mach I

1969-70 Mustang: A Steed for Every Need

The "ponycar" craze waned rapidly during the early 1970s, and the makers of Camaro and Firebird, Cougar and Mustang were forced to adapt to the changed market. Ford Division's response eventually appeared in the 1974 Mustang II, which was a minor-leaguer compared to its predecessors, though it sold well and was a good marketing idea.

Ford's offerings for 1969–70—the last years of its true ponycar—are what interest Mustang lovers. Much of the impetus for them came during the short-lived presidency of Semon E. "Bunkie" Knudsen, who came to Ford in early 1968 after a long career at General Motors. Though Knudsen was replaced within two

years (first by a triumvirate, shortly afterwards by Lee Iacocca), he brought a new spirit of high-performance to Ford Division.

The '69 Mustang kept the 108-inch wheelbase that had been used since 1965, but was larger in most every other dimension. It was vividly restyled, with four more inches of hood, a chunkier silhouette, quad head-lamps, and clean fender lines, all integrated into a recognizably "Mustang" overall look. Underneath the new body was a modified frame, with the crossmember relocated under the front seat to open up badly needed rear seat legroom.

Model offerings took three forms: sporty economy,

luxury tourer, and high-speed muscle machine. With an eye on the premium-ponycar market being exploited by the Pontiac Firebird and Mercury Cougar, Ford released the Grandé hardtop, listed at about $230 more than the standard Mustang hardtop. Standard features included a vinyl-covered roof, color-keyed outside rearview mirrors, wire wheel covers, additional bright trim, subtle beltline striping, imitation teakwood interior paneling, and about 55 extra pounds of sound insulation. Available with either a six or V-8 engine, it accounted for over 22,000 sales.

With an eye to the performance buyer, Ford trotted out the Mach I fastback for '69, with a base price of $3139. Its individual styling touches included simulated air scoops on the rear fenders, a decklid spoiler, and functional hood scoop. A broad, flat hood with matte-black paint and competition hold-downs combined with a sweeping roof to create the look of a genuine performance car. But there was more to it than looks: a standard 351-cubic-inch V-8 with 250 bhp

gave the Mach I terrific performance. Derived from the 289/302 small-block, it was a new engine in many ways, particularly in the shape of its combustion chambers. Though heavier than the 302, it was considerably lighter than the big-block Cobra Jet, and was ideal for the light Mustang chassis. The CJ-428 was the unquestioned drag-strip champ, of course. A Mach I with this option would turn 13.5-second standing-start quarter-miles.

All Mustangs were more potent for 1969 thanks to a much wider engine lineup. It included a new "performance" six, a 250-cid, 155-bhp unit available for just $39 extra. The V-8s ran from the 220-bhp 302 to the big CJ-428, available with or without ram-air induction. The Mach I's standard 351 was available as an option for other models.

Ford released an even more potent Mustang at mid-model year, the Boss 302. A direct answer to the Camaro Z-28, it was Ford's contender in the Sports Car Club of America's Trans-Am series for production

1969 Mustang Boss 302

1969 Mustang Boss 302

1969 Mustang "SportsRoof" Fastback (prototype)

1969 Mustang Convertible

1969 Mustang Grandé Hardtop

1969 Mustang Mach I

"sedans." To qualify the car as a production model Ford was required to build 1000 copies, but ended up producing almost 2000. Though the Boss was a great showroom traffic-builder, its real mission was competition. Two were prepared for the '69 season by Shelby American as the official factory entries. Others were prepped by independents receiving encouragement and technical assistance straight from Dearborn. Boss 302s dominated the Trans-Am in both 1969 and '70.

Styling for the Boss 302 was the work of Larry Shinoda, who had followed Knudsen from GM to Ford. Shinoda's touches were clearly race-oriented—a front air dam and rear spoiler, both effective at speeds above 40 mph, were the most obvious. Matte-black rear window slats, resembling those of the Lamborghini Miura, were of no aerodynamic value, but they looked great. The Boss engine was a 302 tuned to produce a claimed 290 bhp, though that was just for show: dyno testing put it as high as 400. It had the now-famous "Cleveland" heads with oversize intake

valves and huge 1.75-inch exhaust valves inclined in big ports to improve fuel flow. Other features were an aluminum high-rise manifold, Holley four-barrel carb, dual-point ignition, solid lifters, bolted central main bearings, forged crankshaft, and special racing pistons. The chassis was also very special. It came from the factory equipped with ultra-stiff springs, staggered shocks, a Stout CJ four-speed gearbox, power brakes with 11.3-inch front discs and heavy-duty rear drums, and Goodyear F60 × 15 Polyglas tires.

While the Boss was designed for racing, the Mach I was designed for sales. The results during the first half of 1969 are interesting. Out of 184,000 Mustangs delivered, close to 46,000 were Mach Is. The posh Grandé, by comparison, totaled only 15,000. Ford Division general manager John Naughton thus decided to emphasize performance even more by adding the yet hairier Boss 429 to the lineup for mid-1969 and offering "Boss" backlight louvers and rear spoilers as options for any 1970 Mustang "SportsRoof" fastback.

1970 Mustang Mach I

1970 Mustang Boss 302

1970 Mustang Boss 302

1970 Mustang "SportsRoof" Fastback

1970 Mustang "SportsRoof" Fastback

1970 Mustang Hardtop

1970 Mustang Grandé Hardtop

1970 Mustang Mach I

1971 Mustang Boss 351

1971 Mustang Mach I

Ford said the '70 Boss was "even Bossier." And it was. It was the last of the great Mustang *gran turismos,* faster than the '69 on both the curves and the straights. One of its new features was a Hurst shifter, the first ever offered by Ford in a production car.

Mach I engines for 1970 ranged from the 351 two-barrel up to the four-barrel 428 with ram-air. The "Cleveland" powerplant was further refined by a canted-valve cylinder head, larger intake and exhaust ports, and a block and rods designed for extreme durability. The suspension acquired a rear stabilizer bar, which combined with moderate spring rates for a decent ride. The '70 Mach I had its own special grille as well as the matte-black hood paint, twist hood locks, air scoop, twin mirrors, and honeycomb rear panel appliqué from '69.

The Grandé returned for 1970, but Ford made less fuss about it. Perhaps as a result, the model notched only 13,581 sales. Rounding out the line were the "standard" hardtop, convertible, and fastback, available with sixes or 302 V-8s. But despite a wide range of models, Mustang didn't meet Ford's expectations. Against 300,000 of the '69s, sales of the '70s failed to break 200,000. Convertible production sank below 8000 units.

A new formula was clearly needed, and it arrived in the autumn of 1970 in the most changed Mustang in history. The rebodied '71 was newly styled and much larger—big as a Mustang would ever get. Though wheelbase was longer by just an inch, the car was eight inches longer overall, six inches wider, and some 600 pounds heavier than the 1965 original. Increasingly tough emissions standards spelled the end of some engines, and took the fire out of the ones that were left. It just wasn't the same kind of car. Sales continued to wane, dropping to a low of 125,000 for model year 1972. Ford kept the same basic car through 1973 while working on the smaller, more economical Mustang II.

Thus, the exciting Mustangs, launched with such high hopes for 1969, came to an abrupt end after just two years. Their somewhat premature demise was due not only to managerial decisions, but also to forces other than supply and demand that were affecting the car market for the first time in history. Enthusiasts tend to blame Lee Iacocca for the puffed-up '71, but he actually had little to do with it. Those decisions had been made when Knudsen was still president. Knudsen himself had been pro-performance, as he had been years before at GM. But even he had to face the fact that speed, handling, and a fine competition record were no longer the sales weapons they once were.

After the 1970 season, Ford Motor Company abandoned most of its racing efforts, including NASCAR, USAC, the Trans-Am series, and the international circuits. The company then began turning away from excitement to luxury and "paint-on performance" models that could sell in six-figure quantity. So, the start of a new decade marked the end of an era: Mustang—and Ford itself—would never be the same again.

1952 Lincoln with Ford's first ohv V-8

Big-Block V-8s:
The Power of Greatness

$\mathcal{D}$etroit made a wholesale shift to overhead-valve engines from 1948 to 1955. Oldsmobile and Cadillac beat all rivals to the punch with a high-compression ohv V-8 for 1949. Then Chrysler stunned everybody, including Ford, with its big hemi-head V-8 for 1951.

What could Ford do? Well, it couldn't do much more with the old reliable flathead V-8. The 239.4-cubic-inch version, which had been standardized for the new 1949 Ford, was rated at 100 bhp. Its most recent improvements, such as a new distributor and revised cooling system, were aimed more at ensuring reliability than gaining more power. For the 1952 Ford the flathead's compression was pushed up from 6.8 to 7.2:1, which, in combination with a new camshaft, boosted output from 100 to 110 bhp. To assure normal valve life and proper seating, the valves were fitted

with automatic rotators, a feature usually reserved for heavy-duty truck engines.

But nothing more could be done without a major redesign. If new cylinder heads giving better breathing and a more compact combustion space were put on the existing block, the bottom end would not be able to withstand the increased stress. Ford's director of engineering, Harold T. Youngren, had no illusions about adding to the flathead's production life by making more piecemeal modifications. He also had no interest in preserving it, being an ex-Oldsmobile engineer recently hired by Ernest R. Breech, who was effectively running the company until the day Henry Ford II could be considered experienced enough to take over the reins.

Youngren had Breech's ear and confidence, and had no difficulty in getting a program for a new over-

67

Big-block T-Bird at Daytona

1954 Ford Crestline Country Squire Wagon

1954 Mercury Custom Four-Door Sedan

head-valve V-8 approved, complete with a healthy budget. The man Youngren named to head development was the clear-thinking, fast-talking Victor G. Raviolo. Raviolo had first worked for Ford in 1940–41, but spent the war years on assignment to the aircraft industry before returning to Dearborn in 1945. His experience also included three years with Chrysler, two with Packard, and two with the Van Ranst firm of consulting engineers in Detroit. Assisting him were three Ford faithfuls, Robert Stevenson, Allen Cleveland, and Paul Clayton. Stevenson did most of the detail design. He had come to Ford in 1934 as a draftsman at the River Rouge plant, and by 1945 was the company's top engineer for truck powerplants.

The new program did not involve just one completely new engine, but three: a Ford six, a Ford/Mercury V-8, and a Lincoln V-8. And all were needed—and expected—in the shortest time possible. Initial work was completed in 1948, and the first test engines went on the dynamometer later that year. Before the test phase was concluded, over 400 prototype engines had run the equivalent of nearly a million miles in the laboratory and on the road. By mid-1950, the final specifications were approved for production.

For several reasons, it was decided to introduce the Lincoln unit first. Lincoln, after all, was up against Cadillac and Chrysler in the prestige market, and therefore needed a more modern powerplant to match its competitors. Also, Lincoln was a low-volume product, which meant that the company would gain valuable field experience with the new engine in a more manageable number of cars than if it were launched in the high-volume Ford. As it turned out, both the Ford six and the Lincoln V-8 debuted for 1952.

The Lincoln engine had a 3.80-inch bore and a 3.50-inch stroke for 317.5 cubic inches of displacement. On a 7.5:1 compression ratio it delivered 160 bhp, identical to the output of Cadillac's V-8. Because of its deep crankcase, the engine had a "Y" shape cross section, so it became known as the "Y-block" design. The old flathead mill's three crankshaft main bearings gave way to five mains with a total surface of 47.4 square inches. The crankshaft itself was made of forged steel, stronger than the cast iron previously used. Valves were canted at about 18 degrees above wedge-shaped combustion chambers. The crossflow heads were fed from a single carburetor via gently curved runners, assuring near optimal cylinder filling. Hydraulic valve lifters were adopted to keep valve lash at zero regardless of operating temperature. Thanks to a new pressurized cooling system, capacity could be reduced from 34 to 24 quarts (compared with the old 337-cid Lincoln straight eight, a side-valve unit borrowed from the F-8 Ford truck). Camshaft, rocker arms, and valves were all made by a new shell-molding process, developed by Ford in 1950–51, that resulted in light weight, high precision, and lower cost. The 1952 Lincoln V-8 was also the first power unit to incorporate integral valve guides. The valve stems were inserted directly into holes drilled into the cylinder head, which eliminated a lot of little parts.

The smaller V-8 intended for Ford and Mercury was ready in time for 1954-model introduction. With bore and stroke of 3.39 × 3.30 inches it had a displacement of 239 cubic inches, and delivered 145 bhp on a 7.2:1 compression ratio. This was a little short of performance targets, so a displacement increase to 254 cid was planned for 1955. But then Ford found out Chevrolet was pegging its new '55 V-8 at 265 cubic inches. So, bore was taken out to 3.625 inches for 272 cid and a handsome 182 bhp. Next, came a 292 rendition, with bore again stretched (to 3.75 inches), as the standard powerplant for the 1955 Thunderbird. With an 8.0:1 compression ratio and four-barrel carburetor, it was rated at 193 (with manual gearbox) or 198 bhp (automatic transmission).

When Raviolo determined the Y-block's cylinder spacing, he was aiming for a displacement range of 230 to 320 cubic inches. He aimed too low. The need for even more cubes than this was greater than anticipated, yet the Lincoln size was about the maximum possible.

For 1956, Ford offered a 312-cid Y-block with the Lincoln's 3.80-inch bore and a 3.44-inch stroke. With four-barrel carburetor, 9.0:1 compression, and dual exhausts, it delivered 225 bhp. A high-performance unit with twin four-barrels came in at 260 bhp. The following year, compression ratio was raised to 9.7:1, and peak power shot up to 245 and 270 bhp with single and dual four-barrel carbs, respectively. Ford also released a supercharged version of the 312, mainly for stock car racing. Fitted with a McCulloch centrifugal blower, this engine ran on a lower 8.3:1 compression ratio. Its actual output was at least 325 bhp, though Ford claimed only 300.

Robert Stevenson was named chief engineer of Ford Engine & Foundry in 1957. For the previous year-

190-bhp 272 V-8, 1957

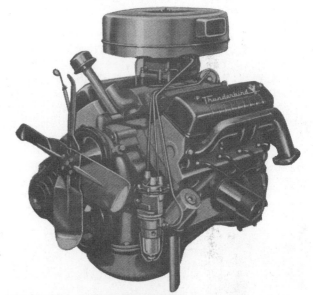

212-bhp "Thunderbird" 292, 1957

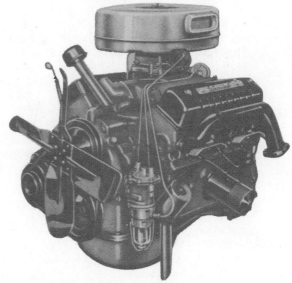

245-bhp "Thunderbird Special" 312 for '57

270-bhp, 1957 "Thunderbird Super" 312 V-8

Mercury's 368 V-8 for '57: 290 bhp

and-a-half he had been working on a replacement for the Y-block. That project led to a whole new engine family known as the FE series. It was derived from the Y-block design, but incorporated all the lessons learned in the field. Cylinder centers were chosen so that enlargement up to 425 cubic inches would be feasible—an arbitrary figure so far above forseeable needs that a long production run seemed assured. The FE's main internal improvements were bigger valves and bigger bearings, the latter allowing the use of a low-cost, precision-cast crankshaft. The first FE engines appeared in Ford Motor Company's 1958

models: 332- and 352-cid units for Ford, a 360 for Mercury, and a 361 for the new medium-priced Edsel. As installed in the Thunderbird, the 352 was rated at an even 300 bhp with four-barrel carburetor and 10.2:1 compression.

Closely related to the FE, but with different block height and connecting rod lengths, was the "MEL" family, which went into production at about the same time. It comprised a 383-cid unit for Mercury and Edsel and a bulldozer 430 for the Lincoln (hence the initials). After the Edsel's demise the MEL V-8s were reserved for FoMoCo's heavyweight luxury models.

'61 Starliner NASCAR stocker

400-bhp "Super Marauder" 430, 1958

'60s Muscle: 1966 390 V-8

Meanwhile, high-performance versions of the FE units were being prepared, beginning with a 360-bhp NASCAR version of the 352 in 1960. Don Sullivan, who had been with Ford since Model T days, played a major role in developing these engines, while Bob Stevenson concentrated on new, larger, mass-production units. A 390-cid FE-series V-8 with 4.05-inch bore and 3.78-inch stroke was introduced for 1961. It was standard for that year's brand-new Thunderbird, where it delivered 300 bhp using a 10.8:1 squeeze and a four-barrel carburetor. This was followed by a 406-cid extension with bore increased to 4.13 inches. It became Ford Division's weapon in the high-performance wars against the Chevy 409 and Chrysler's 413.

Ford next unleashed the unforgettable 427 with a massive 4.24-inch bore and 3.78-inch stroke. Offered as an option for the big Ford Galaxie, it was available with transistorized ignition, and was good for a whopping 410 bhp. In NASCAR trim, it pumped out over 500 bhp. It gave Ford a 1-2-3-4-5 sweep in its very first outing at Daytona in 1963.

Ford also won the NASCAR championship that year thanks to the new big-inch engine. A high-riser version with solid valve lifters and revised lubrication system (side-oiler block) became available in 1964, and dominated stock car racing for the next three seasons. Converted to dry-sump lubrication, it powered the Ford Mark II and Mark IV racers that won the 24 Hours of Le Mans in 1966 and 1967.

A hemi-head conversion of the 427 was designed in 1964 by Norman Faustyn, and became a prime attraction for the drag racing crowd. Despite all-new heads with chain-driven overhead camshafts, engine weight was kept down to about 700 pounds. It was capable of reaching 7200 rpm, and belted out more than 600 bhp on a tight 12.0:1 compression ratio.

From a performance viewpoint, the 427 certainly represented the peak of the FE series' development. Sadly, it was discontinued after 1968. But one big-block production engine would carry on, the 428, introduced in 1966. This retained the basic FE block, but

had a longer-throw crankshaft that gave a 3.98-inch stroke. Bore was pulled back to 4.13 inches. Its main strengths were smoothness and robust low-end torque. This made it much like Lincoln's MEL-series engine, which grew from 430 to 462 cubes (4.38-inch bore and 3.83-inch stroke) for 1966. The 428 was canceled at the end of 1970.

At the lower end of the displacement scale, the old 352 had been discontinued at the end of the 1964 model year. The 390 lasted through 1968, then returned for one year only as an option for the 1971 Ford. Mercury had a 410-cid version of the FE-series V-8 for 1967, combining the 428 crankshaft with the 390's

410-bhp 427 for 1963

1963's High-Performance 427: 425 bhp

4.05-inch bore, but it was a short-lived variant.

By the end of the '60s, rival engines were ganging up on the FE series from both sides. By combining a 4.00-inch stroke with the 4.00-inch bore from the 351 small-block, Ford Engine & Foundry created a relatively efficient 400-cid unit having torque and emission characteristics suitable for a mass-produced family car. It became optional for the 1971 Ford LTD and Mercury Monterey. An even bigger challenge came from the new 385 series, a more modern, lightweight V-8 designed by Albert F. Martin. (It was called 385 series because 3.85 inches was the stroke of the first design.) It began in 1968 as a 460-cid (4.36 × 3.85) Lincoln unit, followed a year later by a 429 (4.36 × 3.59) version for the Thunderbird. Both soon spread to lesser Ford and Mercury models including intermediates.

For 1970, Ford offered the 429 in five states of tune. The base version had a two-barrel carburetor and 10.5:1 compression for a rated 320 bhp. Changing to a four-barrel carburetor boosted output to 360. The Boss 429 had a bigger four-barrel carburetor, 11.0:1 compression, and mechanical valve lifters that resulted in maximum output of 375 bhp (at 5200 rpm). The remaining two were high-performance editions with 11.5:1 compression; one had hydraulic lifters, the other solid tappets. Both delivered between 450 and 500 bhp, and were available for the Torino and Montego strictly for stock car and drag racing. Because weight differences were slight, the 460 replaced the 429 in most applications for 1974, while the small-block 400 took over elsewhere.

Few changes were made to Ford Motor Company's engine families in the wake of the first fuel shock in late 1973. One reason was the company's stubborn reluctance to begin downsizing its cars, a decision made by Henry Ford II himself. Ford, the company, would give in to the inevitable, of course, but not before it was almost too late. Thus it was that the hoary old 460 was still standard in the Lincoln Continental and Mark V and optional for the big Ford and Mercury right up through 1978. But that was its last year.

And that's the end of the big-block V-8 story, except for a final comment. Considering their humble origins these engines lived a remarkably long time. The cars they powered ran the gamut from ordinary to awe-inspiring, from abject failure (Edsel) to astonishing success (GT-40). They were world-beaters in the truest sense. Big-inch engines have all but disappeared from the automotive landscape now. But we'll always remember Ford's big-blocks because of that oft-repeated truth from the bygone age in which they thrived: "There's no substitute for cubic inches!"

A pair of '65 Galaxie stockers lead a NASCAR race.

Above: A "submarine bow" and "flowerpot tail-lights" marked the all-new 1961 T-Bird. Shown is the dashing convertible. Left: The 1962 Sports Roadster answered customer requests for another two-seat Thunderbird. Fiberglass tonneau covered rear seat, and didn't interfere with top operation. Spinner wire wheels and skirtless rear fenders were standard.

Opposite top: "Starlift" hardtop was a proposed option for the 1962 Galaxie convertible, but never materialized. Opposite center and bottom left and right: Ford built just 455 Thunderbird Sports Roadsters for 1963. Curvy cockpit was a feature of all 1961–63 T-Birds. This page: Fairlane 500 Sports Coupe (top) and Falcon Futura convertible (above) were two of the "Lively Ones" for 1963. Left: 1964 Thunderbird convertible, shown with the very rare Sports Roadster conversion.

Top: Fastback roof for "1963½" made the big Galaxie (500XL shown) more competitive on the supertracks. Above left and right: The 1964 Galaxie 500XL was big—and big on sporty luxury—yet was also amazingly durable. Most were ordered with the burly 390 V-8. Right: An elegant new look and "Rolls-Royce" refinement made the '65 500XL a smoother performer. Far right, top: Last year for the rally-proven Falcon Sprint was 1965. Shown is the Futura hardtop. Center: The jaunty hardtop version of the "1964½" Mustang, the car that started the ponycar stampede. Bottom: Mustang 2+2 fastback arrived for the 1965 model year.

Above: Early Mustang convertibles like this 1966 fetch astounding prices nowadays. Below: Ford's ponycar was reskinned for 1967, and got a 390 big-block V-8 option. Right: The Fairlane shed its dowdy looks for 1966, and gained two hot GT models, convertible (shown) and hardtop. Far right, top: New Torino fastback was Ford's performance mid-size for 1968. Good aerodynamics made it a natural for stock-car racing. Center: Torino paced the 1968 Indy 500. Bottom: 1969 Torino Cobra offered brawn on a budget.

Above: The 1968 Shelby GT-500KR packed Ford's mighty Cobra-Jet 428. Naturally, the KR stood for "King of the Road." The '68s were the last of the Shelby-built Mustang GTs. Right: The Torino Cobra returned for 1970 as part of a restyled, less aerodynamic mid-size line. A standard 370-bhp 429 made it the fastest Ford of all that year. Below: The 1970 Mustang was the last of the breed faithful to the spirit of the 1965 original. Mach I shown carries optional 428 V-8 and "shaker" hood scoop. Special appearance touches included twist hood locks and lots of black paint.

1962 Galaxie 500XL Two-Door Hardtop

1962~65 Galaxie 500XL: Full-Size Flyer

*C*ar enthusiasts say funny things. A few years ago, one buff magazine concluded that Ford management "didn't feel completely comfortable about any of their full-sized cars until they came out with the all-new quiet-riding '65." If true, there must have been some very nervous managers in Dearborn before then.

Actually, the big Fords did quite well in the early '60s. Through 1964, the standard Chevys never outsold their Ford counterparts by a ratio of more than 1¾ to 1,

and in 1961 and '64 the margin was much less than that. As for Ford's redesigned '65 big cars, Impala and company outnumbered them (including the LTD) by nearly two to one. Because the industry usually views the annual "production race" in calendar year terms, we usually fail to note that, overall, Ford outsold Chevy in the 1961 model year. So the 1960–64 Fords couldn't have been *that* worrisome.

The design and engineering concepts of the early-

1960 Galaxie Starliner Hardtop

Race-prepping the 1960 Starliner

1961 Galaxie Starliner Hardtop

1962 Galaxie Two-Door Sedan

1962 Galaxie with "Starlift" top

"Starlift" top, proposed '62 option

Norm Nelson's '62 Galaxie USAC stocker

'60s full-size Fords go back to the 1958 model year, when the 332- and 352-cid "big-block" V-8s were first introduced. Although the AMA decision not to condone racing was then in force, the '58 Ford made a pretty good racing car. Private competitors began showing up at the tracks with the lighter Tudor models fitted with these big-block engines, and captured 16 NASCAR Grand Nationals in 1958. But it wasn't enough to take the title from Chevy, which won 23 (though Ford was number one in USAC). In 1960, Ford's 10 NASCAR

Don White's '62 Galaxie USAC stocker

Fred Lorenzen with '62 NASCAR Galaxie

wins plus the Thunderbird's six was two better than Chevy's combined total of 14.

But the product planning people under Robert McNamara weren't interested in racing. The full-size 1959–61 Ford was conventional, bordering on dull: forgettable styling, flat bench seat, and large but mildly tuned engines. This reflected the success Thunderbird was enjoying (90,000 sales in 1960) and also McNamara's single-minded devotion to building only profitable products. Let Fords be uninteresting, just as long as they sell. Although he had personally sold management on the bucket-seat "personal-luxury" four-seater idea, McNamara was not eager to put bucket seats and high style into Ford's big cars, which could be sold at $1000 or so less than a Bird.

All this would change by mid-1962 for two reasons. First, McNamara was replaced in 1960 as Ford Division general manager by the savvy Lee Iacocca. Iacocca liked the Thunderbird, but also wanted to add some muscle to the standard Ford's physique. Second, the public was starting to go crazy over bucket seats, floorshifts, and other "sports car" features—and not just on small models like the Corvair Monza. The first of the Super Sport Chevy 409s in 1961 was not a stupendous seller, but it cast a performance image over the whole Chevy line that hadn't been seen since 1957. Thus, Chevy had a distinct edge with performance-conscious buyers over Ford, which for 30 years had been viewed as the leader in low-cost performance.

One of Iacocca's favorite sales tools was (and still is) the "fractional" model year ("1962½," "1963½," and so on). Mid-model year coincides with the traditional spring selling season, when dealers like to have something "new" to stimulate showroom traffic after the lazy winter selling months. Sometimes, a mid-year introduction was used to give a new car a strong sendoff, as in the case of the first Mustang, a '65 model launched six months in advance of the formal model year. Other mid-year introductions were simply late entries considered part of the model year that began the previous fall, but were still important new products. In this latter category was the Galaxie 500XL, which arrived in the spring of 1962 as a "1962½" model along with a bevy of spruced-up Falcons and Fairlanes, all advertised under "The Lively Ones" theme.

While the base engine in the big Ford at that time was a 223-cid six, the XL's standard powerplant was a 292 V-8 with 170 bhp. Two big-block engines were optional, the 352 and 390, the latter offering up to 401 bhp. Those who liked to stir their own gears could get a Borg-Warner four-speed gearbox or a three-speed with overdrive, but the typical drivetrain was the 300-bhp 390 teamed with Cruise-O-Matic shiftless transmission. Nevertheless, the availability of four-on-the-floor and extra horses had strong implications for the track.

Ford also had the king-size 406, introduced after the start of the '62 model year. Basically a 390 bored out by .08 inch, it delivered 385 bhp with standard four-barrel Holley carburetor. Three two-barrels were available to bring it up to 405, about one bhp per cubic inch. The 406 enabled Ford to capture six NASCAR Grand National stock car wins in 1962—not a lot. The stockers were based on the lighter, fixed-pillar Tudor sedan body, not the fancy XL hardtop. Still, Pontiac's 421-cid racers were quicker. This was partly due to Ford's 1962 restyle, which decreed a squared-off, Thunderbird-type roof for the big cars. This attempt to tie the big Fords more closely to the fashionable Bird thus eliminated the more aerodynamic "Starliner" fastback hardtop, offered for 1960–61, which had found favor on the track. (Ford briefly toyed with the idea of making a bolt-on Starliner-type hardtop available for the Galaxie convertible, ostensibly a production option but really intended for racing. The name "Starlift" was chosen, but the top was vetoed by NASCAR.)

While no threat on the big ovals, the 500XL was the sportiest of the full-size Fords, with the best the Division had in the way of luxury and power. There were two models, Victoria two-door hardtop (base price $3268) and Sunliner convertible ($3518). Some 40,000 were sold, including 13,183 soft-tops. Such sprightly sales owed much to the car's comfort and good looks. The interior, unique to the XL, offered front bucket seats, a "buckety" rear bench, center console, and custom door panels. Deep carpeting, chrome-plated dash controls, a large array of courtesy lights, deluxe armrests, padded sunvisors, Mylar trim ac-

1963 Galaxie 500 XL Two-Door Hardtop

'63 Galaxie "slantbacks" in USAC action

cents, and metal-trimmed pedal pads were also part of the package. The exterior was stock except for special emblems and wheel covers. Buyers could opt for wire wheel covers and even leather inserts for the bucket seats.

Dave Lundman's '63 "slantback" USAC stocker

Fred Lorenzen's '64 Galaxie for NASCAR

1964 Galaxie 500XL Convertible

Retaining the inner body structure from 1960–62, Ford reskinned its big cars for '63 with new outer panels and a new roof. A four-door hardtop joined the XL sub-series. Model year production was 12,596 four-doors, 29,713 two-doors, and 18,551 convertibles. Spring saw a new "1963½" semi-fastback two-door hardtop with a cleaner, more tapered roof that was aerodynamically superior to the T-Bird-style notch-back. Ford sold 33,870 of these "fastbacks" (and another 100,000 in regular Galaxie 500 trim) despite the mid-year introduction, making this the most popular of the four XL body styles for '63.

Important engine changes were made for 1963 as well. First, the old 292 was replaced as the base XL powerplant by a 289; then the 406 was bored out to 427 cid, displacement right at the NASCAR limit. With drag strip and stock car oval in mind, Ford offered the 427 in two stages of tune: 410 bhp with four-barrel carb and optional transistorized ignition or 425 bhp with two matched four-barrels. For the strip, an S/S kit was added to the option list, consisting of fiberglass body panels that shaved over 160 pounds off the front end. Ford even built a few cars with the S/S kit and stripped interiors at the factory. Despite such goings on, the typical 1963 XL rolled out the door by means of a Thunderbird 390 engine and automatic.

Though not too successful at the drags against the Super/Stock Mopars, the big Ford enjoyed one of its best NASCAR seasons in 1963. Commencing with Dan Gurney's win at the Riverside 500 in January, Fords were in the winner's circle at every 500-mile race, and won 23 Grand Nationals in all.

For one last time, 1964, Ford Division reskinned its 1960 full-size bodyshell. A Quality Control Program instituted in 1961 had by now achieved satisfying results. Historically, the '64 Ford may not seem significant—basically just a five-year-old design set to be phased out for the all-new 1965s, the most changed Ford passenger cars since 1949. But for collectors, it is perfect. Wrote Tim Howley in *Special-Interest Autos* magazine: "The '64 Ford stands quite alone as the ultimate Total Performance Ford."

Howley called the '64 evolutionary, but noted that it

The '64 XL's bucket-seat interior

Prototype 427 V-8 for '64 XL

reached near perfection in the process. Though mechanical specs were basically the same as in 1963, "styling had been carefully dictated by the aerodynamics of racing. Even the body panels were designed to be lighter than the '63s." There were three 500XL models: the convertible and two- and four-door hardtops both with the fastback roof from 1963½. Production totaled 58,306 two-doors, 15,169 convertibles, and 14,661 four-doors. Evidently the public agreed with *Motor Trend* magazine, which gave its "Car of the Year" honors to the entire 1964 Ford line, including the full-size models. Because of the strong quality-control effort, XLs and other big Fords wore like iron. "With that kind of quality," according to Howley, "all too many of them were driven for 10 years or 200,000 miles, and they just don't show their age. Rare is the low-mileage '64 XL, as this was not the kind of car you bought to put away in your garage."

In an age where teenagers get their kicks matching Toyota Liftbacks at stop light *grands prix,* the performance of the '64 500XL seems awesome today. In a contemporary magazine comparison test of 390- and

1964 (upper) and '65 (lower) XL stockers

1965 Galaxie 500XL Two-Door Hardtop

1965 Galaxie 500XL Convertible

427-cid models, the milder car did 0–60 mph in 9.3 seconds, which is fair going, but the 427 clocked it in 7.4 seconds—remarkable for a two-ton, full-size car that could only be described as luxurious.

No engine mods were made on the '64s, nor was advertised output boosted on any power team. Ford's drag racing colors were now carried by the lighter and more competitive Fairlane. But the big cars still ran in the Grand Nationals, and did well. Chrysler Corporation brought back its fabled hemi-head V-8 for the '64 campaign, planning to beat the stuffing out of any GM or Ford challenger. Ford told NASCAR this was unfair. If Chrysler could race the hemi, Ford ought to be allowed to use its overhead-cam 427. Not quite, NASCAR replied, but the non-ohc 427 could have a high-rise manifold and a higher rev limit, both of which Ford quickly attended to. The hemis grabbed the limelight: Plymouth won the Daytona 500 and the World 600 at Charlotte, NC. Mopars also finished 1-2-3 at the Darlington 500. But when the smoke cleared, Ford was still the star of the show: 30 NASCAR victories.

Ford had its greatest NASCAR year ever in 1965, winning 48 of the scheduled 55 events. Although a rules dispute kept the factory Plymouth and Dodge teams out for most of the season, these and other makes were still represented by intermediates—which makes the big Ford's track record all the more impressive. Veteran Ford pilot Fred Lorenzen won that year's prestigious Daytona 500, averaging 141.539 mph in a rain-shortened race. Bobby Johns placed third, also in a Galaxie. Of course, the stockers bore little resemblance to the all-new showroom models, now billed as being "quieter than a Rolls-Royce." Pride of the line was the limousine-like LTD, and all big Fords acquired more square-cut body lines. Yet the 500XL hardtop

retained its semi-fastback roofline from 1963–64, and this undoubtedly contributed to Ford's victory streak on the supertracks.

By 1966 the demand for burly big cars was winding down. Big-inch intermediates and sporty compacts were now the tire-burner's favorites. Ford's Fairlane was all-new that year, and could now accommodate big-block V-8s. Ford began the NASCAR season with the Galaxie, sat out most of it because of a rules hassle, then returned for the finale with the Fairlanes. On the production side, 1966 brought the new Galaxie 500 7-Litre, offered in hardtop and convertible styles with a low-output version of the big 428. Designed for smoothness rather than brute power, it offered a rated 345 bhp in standard tune or 360 optional. It was not popular, though, and faded into oblivion after 1967.

Despite their race triumphs, Ford's big cars were clearly aimed more at luxury than performance after 1966. The hairy big-block engines hardly fitted the posh image the Division wanted for these models, yet the 427 was available through 1968 (replaced at mid-year by a hot 428). So, too, was the 500XL, which continued as the separate XL series right on through 1970. While these later versions lacked the all-out performance of the 1962–65 XLs, they still offered plenty of punch despite their increased weight and size and the choking effects of emissions controls.

Ford built quite a few of the fast and spirited XLs, so a fair number survive today. Twenty years after the first one rolled off the line, the XL seems much too big and much too thirsty. Still, $30 worth of premium may not be too high a price for a Sunday drive in one of these "Total Performance" Fords. An increasing number of enthusiasts would agree. For them, an XL makes "getting there" *more* than half the fun.

Fred Lorenzen's '65 XL in NASCAR action

1966 Galaxie 500XL Convertible

1967 Galaxie 500XL Fastback

1968 Torino GT Convertible

1963-70 Fairlane and Torino GT: Mid-Size Muscle Machines

*F*ord's thin-wall small-block V-8 was, as pointed out elsewhere in this book, one of the firm's great engineering achievements. Aside from the efficiency of its basic design, this gem of an engine had great potential for more displacement and more performance. By 1963, Ford was wringing almost 1 bhp per cubic inch from its bored-out 289-cid descendant. By 1968, it had been bored out again—to 302 cid—and reworked to meet federal emissions standards for the next five years. Though it was rumored that pistons on the early 260-cid units tended to seek daylight too readily, all the basic design bugs were squashed with the 289. This outstanding engine family would see wide application at Ford Motor Company for some two decades, right on into the 1980s.

The new lightweight V-8 had been designed specifically for the new intermediate Ford Fairlane, and arrived with it for 1962. A 271-bhp high-performance 289 was offered as early as 1963. It didn't really make a "muscle car" out of the Fairlane, though specially prepared versions had enjoyed modest success at drag races. Then Pontiac dumped its Bonneville 389 into the mid-size 1964 Tempest to produce the GTO—and blew the Fairlane and just about everything else into the proverbial weeds.

Ford couldn't let such a challenge go unanswered, so Dearborn's potent 427 soon found its way into the Fairlane. But because the car's engine bay wasn't wide enough for the big-block, engineers had to improvise. What they developed was the "Thunderbolt" package, available on a *very* limited basis. This consisted of lightweight fiberglass bumpers and body panels, Plexiglas windows, and a modified chassis that allowed the 427 to be shoehorned in. The finished product resembled the nondescript Fairlane two-door sedan, but that's where the similarity ended. Thunderbolts proved a decent match for the thumping GTOs and muscular Mopars in drag racing's Super/Stock class, but that's as far as it went. There still wasn't a performance Fairlane for the street.

For 1963, the Fairlane 500 series had acquired a special version of the two-door hardtop called the Sport Coupe. Like the Falcon Futura and Galaxie 500XL, it was one of Ford's new mid-year "Lively Ones," with bucket seats and a plush interior. Over 28,000 were sold—encouraging if not sensational. Sales remained at about this level for 1964–65. One problem was the car's uninspired styling. That was rectified for 1966 when Fairlane got a new, longer body with crisp, flowing lines. Also new were four sporty XL

1966 Fairlane 500 Hardtop

Mario Andretti's Fairlane at Daytona

Fred Lorenzen's Fairlane in a pit stop

1967 Fairlane 500XL Hardtop

1967 Fairlane 500XL GT Convertible

models: a convertible and hardtop offered in standard and fancier GT trim. The GTs came with the 315-bhp 390 V-8. Automatic transmission, which was usually ordered, made the designation GTA. The top engine option and potential GTO-equalizer was a 335-bhp 390, which gave the typical GTA a quarter-mile time of just 15 seconds.

Unfortunately, Pontiac had also been busy, and offered the GTO with as much as 360 bhp the same year. But the Fairlane's 1966 restyle brought a wider engine room, so now Ford could easily shove in any engine it wanted to. Not surprisingly, a 427 option appeared midway through the model year. However, it came too late to halt Pontiac's dominance of the Super/Stock class, and was really overkill for the street. By contrast, the Fairlane 390 was a much more tractable car, and its performance was certainly nothing to be ashamed of.

Ford couldn't duplicate its great 1965 NASCAR record in 1966, mainly because the Petty Plymouths were starting to weave a long skein of success. Plymouth was again champion in 1967, but not before Ford had switched from running Galaxies to Fairlanes. Dearborn took home 10 Grand National trophies.

The 500XL became a separate Fairlane series for 1967, but offered the same four models. The ragtops are extremely rare. Ford built only 1943 XL convertibles and 2117 GT versions for the model year. The hardtops were much more numerous—14,871 and 18,670, respectively. The production 427 offered 410 or 425 bhp. A sole 390-bhp version was listed on the Fairlane's initial '68 option sheet, but got the hook after a few months in favor of the new Cobra Jet 428, which had the advantage of complying with federal emissions standards.

The XL was dropped for 1968. The new top of the line was a Fairlane offshoot called Torino. The series comprised the same six body styles, including a wagon and four-door sedan. There were three Torino GTs: convertible (again rare: 5310 built) and notchback and fastback two-door hardtops. With NASCAR pilots switching from full-size to intermediate-size mounts, Ford felt obliged to improve its cars' winability, and the slippery fastback helped, particularly on the big southern ovals. David Pearson's Fairlane was national champion that year, and Ford won 20 Grand Nationals. In USAC racing it was the same story, with A. J. Foyt's Fairlane on top. In ARCA (Auto Racing Club of America), Benny Parsons was tops in a Torino.

For 1969, the Torino line and its three GT models returned. The standard GT engine was the 302 V-8, with the 390 optional. An interesting newcomer was the Torino Cobra, a low-bucks muscle car patterned after the Plymouth Road Runner. A detrimmed fastback, it had the CJ-428 engine, four-speed transmission, and heavy-duty suspension standard, all for only $3139. The Torino Cobra lived up to its racy looks on the dragstrips, where it proved to be the fastest Ford intermediate yet. Its typical quarter-mile time was 14.5 seconds, and the 0–60 mph run took a mere six seconds flat.

Ford had its last big NASCAR year in 1969. Before it began, Richard Petty was enticed to the Dearborn camp after a 10-year allegiance to Plymouth. The likely reason was what Ford had up its sleeve. Named Talladega after the newly opened Alabama speedway, it was a Torino fastback with wind-tunnel-tested body modifications. Its smooth front end, flush grille, and special front bumper (actually a stock Torino rear bumper) gave better aerodynamics, so top speed went up without any powertrain changes.

Ford sought approval for a special 429 with crescent-shaped cylinder heads. After an initial argument, NASCAR allowed it. So equipped, the Talladega proved formidable on the high-speed tracks. Richard Petty won his first time out, at the Riverside 500. Lee Roy Yarborough was victorious at the Daytona 500. David Pearson ended up with the NASCAR crown, and Ford won 26 Grand Nationals—a record never equalled.

The Torino was overhauled for 1970, with more curvaceous lines and a one-inch-longer wheelbase. Profiles were lower and five inches longer than in 1969. The same treatment was applied to the companion Fairlane 500 sedan, hardtop, and wagon. There were also stripped editions of this trio called Falcon, introduced at mid-model year. There were 11 Torino models including a GT hardtop and convertible and the Cobra fastback with the CJ-429 engine and four-speed gearbox.

Unfortunately for the racers, the '70 Torino was not such a good deal. Though it looked more wind-cheating, the restyled roof actually *cut* top speed by 5 mph. NASCAR contestants stayed with their "used" '69 models. Meanwhile, Dodge and Plymouth had their ultra-slippery Charger Daytona and Superbird, so the season turned out to be a Mopar show. Only six races fell to Ford in 1970, and Torino drivers were further discouraged by a big cut in the firm's competition budget.

'67 Fairlane stocker in Daytona pits

1968 Torino GT Fastback

1968 Torino Hardtop

The 1970 "street" Torinos were still impressive performers. There were no fewer than four Boss 429 engines available offering 360 to 375 horsepower. The 370-bhp Torino Cobra retained its position as the fastest model in the Ford line. Its new standard muscle

A. J. Foyt's '69 Talladega in 1971

dropped the power-to-weight ratio to only 10.5 lbs/bhp, the lowest since the '66 GTA. Zero to 60 in six seconds and quarter-mile ETs of 14–14.5 seconds were available right off the showroom floor.

But the times, they were a'changing. Though 429s were still available for 1971, the Cobra was downgraded to a standard 351 V-8, and horsepower was down almost all across the engine chart. Ford won only three NASCAR events for the year. The 1972 models brought another redesign, with heavier body-on-frame construction instead of a unitized structure and coil springs instead of leafs for the rear suspension. There were now two wheelbase lengths, 114 inches for two-doors and 118 on four-door models. The Cobra was no more, and the sole "performance" models were the Gran Torino Sport notchback and fastback hardtops. Ford was now emphasizing luxury and comfort; factory-backed racing was a thing of the fuel-plentiful past. Indicative of the trend was the once-mighty 429, now detuned to a lowly 205 bhp net so it could run on regular-grade gas. The Torino fastback was elimi-nated after 1973, and the name itself was scrubbed after 1976 in favor of . . . LTD II.

From the historian's viewpoint, the "Total Performance" intermediates were not a major contribution to Ford Division's success in the '60s, because they never sold in very high numbers. However, from the enthusiast's viewpoint, they are among Ford's best design and engineering efforts of the era, cars equally at home on road and track alike. The 1966–67 Fairlane 500XLs, GTs, and GTAs were beautifully styled and well built, competent in corners, and as fast as any sane person could want. The Torino Cobra was an affordable street-stocker that could show its tail to just about any rival up to, and possibly including, a full-house GTO. Fairlanes and Torinos were responsible for rescuing Ford in NASCAR once the Galaxies were rendered too large and uncompetitive.

So, these mid-size muscle machines go into our book as great cars from Ford. Their excitement makes them easy to remember; their excellence makes them hard to forget.

1969 Torino GT Fastback

1969 Torino Cobra

1969 Torino GT Convertible

1970 Torino Cobra

1970 Torino Cobra

1970 Torino GT Fastback

"Shelby Mk IV" protoype for De Tomaso Mangusta

Powered by Ford: A World of "Total Performance"

Remember "Total Performance?" It was one of Ford's best-known advertising themes of the '60s, those turbulent high-flying years when "hot" cars ruled the road. Of course, other automakers had slogans, but "Total Performance" was not just hype. It described not only Ford's flashy, big-engine, production cars, but also its commitment to racing. The result was nothing less than an all-out assault on all areas of motorsport.

It was a time when Fords and Ford-powered cars were everywhere: the Cosworth V-8 engine in Formula One, the Indy-Fords in USAC, the GT-40 in international endurance racing, the Holman-Moody and Bill Stroppe stockers in NASCAR, the Falcon Sprint in international rallying, the Shelby Cobra and GT-350 in SCCA's A-production and B-production classes. The world had never seen anything like it. "Total Performance" was an enormously profitable—and quite expensive—undertaking. It brought not only "the thrill of victory," but also inestimable prestige and publicity, all of which undoubtedly contributed to Ford's strong sales in these years. Competition also brought a wealth of engineering knowledge and experience, some of which would benefit later Ford production models.

But "Powered by Ford" was already a tradition long

Cobra 289s for strip and street

Factory 1964–65 Cobra 289 drag racer

Cobra Daytona Coupe

before that legend appeared on the fenders of cars like the Shelby Cobras. Beginning with the famous flathead V-8 of the '30s, Ford engines gained a reputation for simplicity, reliability, and adaptability that endeared them to hop-up artists everywhere. A souped-up flathead bolted into a cut-down Model A roadster was the classic formula for a hot rod in the '40s and '50s. A welter of aftermarket speed equipment made it easy to wring more juice out of a flathead or one of Ford's later ohv V-8s. And because so many of these engines were made, a good one at a dirt cheap price was as close as your nearest junkyard.

In this chapter we take a look at four interesting cars from the "Total Performance" years, all Powered by Ford. Two, the A.C. Cobra 289/427 and the De Tomaso Pantera, are hybrids—an American engine transplanted into an existing car designed and built by a foreign manufacturer. Another, the Shelby-Mustang, is a modified version of a high-volume domestic model, and recalls a good many of the short-lived minor makes in the early postwar years. The fourth, the mid-engine Ford GT, is perhaps the best example of the sheer enthusiasm for motorsports that permeated Ford in the '60s.

There are many other Ford-powered cars we could describe, but can't for lack of space. Some readers will no doubt note the singular omission of the British-built Sunbeam Tiger, which got its considerable urge from a Ford 260 V-8. However, this was not really a great car from Ford—it was a great car from Chrysler, which bought Sunbeam's parent company (Rootes Group) after the model was already in production. The Tiger put Chrysler in the awkward position of advertising and having to warranty a car with a Ford engine, which probably explains why it was discontinued shortly after the takeover.

So, fasten your seatbelts as we recall four fabulous performance machines—all exciting, all world-beaters, all Powered by Ford.

A.C. Cobra

The most striking thing about the Cobras was their speed: they were the fastest street sports cars ever produced. A well-tuned Cobra 289 would do 0–100 mph in 14 seconds. The 427-engine model would do 0–100 mph—*and back to 0*—in 14 seconds. No other car sold straight off a showroom floor was their equal for performance.

The Cobra story is one chapter in the saga of Carroll Shelby, America's best-known independent sports car entrepreneur. Retired as a race driver in 1960, Shelby had set his heart on building an American-engine car that could compete with the most sophisticated V-12 racing machines the Europeans could muster.

The Cobra's basic body, beautiful and lithe, had

been in production as the A.C. Ace since 1953. Its rock-solid tubular chassis had four-wheel independent suspension, and was an ideal candidate for a Ford V-8 transplant. Though it bore the badge of A.C. Cars (Thames Ditton, Surrey, England), the Cobra was a genuine hybrid. A. C. built the bodies and chassis, then shipped them to California where Shelby installed the thin-wall Ford 289 V-8. The two Cobra prototypes initially constructed were powered by 260 V-8s supplied by none other than Lee Iacocca. After the first 75 production cars, Shelby changed to the high-performance 289, which he eventually coaxed from 271 to 380 horsepower by means of four Weber carbs, a special head, and a full-race camshaft. The Ace's styling was slightly changed by extending the nose a bit to accommodate the Ford engine. Steering was also changed—for the better—to a Shelby-designed rack-and-pinion system.

The Cobra's 1962 base price seems almost incredible now: $5995, just slightly more than a Corvette. Though Shelby's ambition had been to build a car able to beat Ferrari and Corvette in competition, he had also created a magnificent street sports car. It may have been spartan, its weather protection crude, but its lines were rakishly elegant, and it simply ran away from Corvettes, Ferraris, and Jaguars on every kind of road.

With assistance from former Sting Ray designer Pete Brock and racing experts Ken Miles and Phil Remington, Shelby prepared a team of racing Cobras that appeared in SCCA events in 1963. Bob Johnson won the A-production championship for Shelby, and Bob Holbert captured the manufacturer's division of the U.S. Road Race of Champions. The Cobra couldn't beat the light Corvette Grand Sport racers at the Nassau Speed Weeks, but after 1964 it owned class A-production. During 1963–64, Pete Brock built the Kammtailed Cobra Daytona coupes that ran 1-2-3-5-7 at Sebring and finished fourth at Le Mans. Cobras kept running and winning through 1966, by which time Shelby had switched from building 289s to the unbelievable 427s.

The 427's 0–100–0 mph performance, "ordinary" off-the-floor stuff, demands perspective. It can perhaps best be appreciated by noting that, in 1964, Aston Martin was claiming 25 seconds for the same feat. In straightline acceleration the 427 was astonishing: 0–60 mph in 4.5 seconds, 0–100 mph in 8.7. It had a stronger frame than the 289, coil instead of leaf springs, and fatter tires. Even so, it was a demon for even the very best drivers, and downright dangerous for everyone else.

For these reasons and more, the Cobra 427 is the most desirable American sports car ever built. In 1967, you could buy one for what a timid, mildly optioned Ford EXP costs today: $7000. Nowadays, even a less-than-perfect example runs at least $40,000. Quantities are limited: only 356 were made. The smaller-engine Cobra 289 is more numerous: 855, counting 27 late-production models that used the 427 body. The 289 doesn't handle as well as the 427, which is a beastly thing itself, but it takes less effort to steer and brake. It really is a wonderful car to drive, lightning quick and gratifyingly reponsive in the right hands. Going for between $25,000 and $30,000 today in good condition, the 289 Cobra will continue to appreciate in value each year as the memorable age of Carroll Shelby fades further into the past.

Ford GT

The 24 hours of Le Mans is the world's most prestigious automobile race. At the height of its competition awareness, Ford Motor Company set out to win it. No American car in postwar history had ever won the French endurance classic, although one, the Cunningham, had come close.

England's Eric Broadley, designer of the Lola GT, was contracted to create a sports-racing car built around Ford's thin-wall small-block V-8. At the same time, Ford also signed former Aston Martin racing manager John Wyer to manage its racing team and Caroll Shelby to act as an advisor. Broadley's GT-40 (so designated because it measured just 40 inches high) was ready by early 1964. Its "Indy" engine, mounted behind the driver, was very special—aluminum block, four Weber carburetors, and 350 bhp. Its displacement was slightly below that of the standard 260 to keep it at the 4.1-liter (256.3-cid) limit then in force. Ford raced GT-40s during the 1964 season, but never with real success. Broadley was dropped, and Carroll Shelby was asked to perfect the car.

By this time, Shelby had had ample experience with his Cobra. His first move was to replace the Indy V-8

Fort GT-40

1968 Ford Mark III ("street" GT-40)

with the more reliable 289 Cobra engine. He also modified the car's Colotti gearbox (chosen by Broadley) to cure its reliability problems, which had been the main cause of trouble in 1964. Shelby American engineers also installed oversize ventilated disc brakes. By mid-1965 they had achieved the reliability Ford knew was essential for winning long-distance events.

It was soon determined that to win at Le Mans the GT-40 needed a larger engine than the 289. The car was accordingly reengineered in Dearborn to accept the big 427 NASCAR unit, then putting out 500 bhp in competition tune. In this form, the Ford GTs ran at Le Mans '65, but again proved a disappointment. Despite a strong start in which they led the entire field, all the cars retired during the race, again because of gearbox trouble.

Ford instituted a competition of its own, between Shelby and the Holman & Moody people, to reengineer and improve the cars still further for Le Mans 1966. Eight factory sponsored entries, all 427-powered, showed up on race day, backed by five more GTs entered by private teams. Although the rigors of the race eliminated 10 of the cars during the race, Ford nevertheless had its finest hour in international competition. The three remaining GT-40s—two Shelbys and one Holman & Moody, in that order—finished first, second, and third overall! Ford had won a race previously considered the preserve of the great European marques, a brilliant achievement in American automotive history. And just to prove this was no fluke, the GTs came back the following year to win Le Mans once again.

The lithe, potent, and now reliable GT-40s continued to enjoy success after Ford officially ended its factory sponsorship of the cars following the '67 Le Mans victory. One GT, usually driven by Jackie Ickx and Brian Redman and entered by the Gulf Oil racing team, finished first overall in four major international races during 1968. As a private entry, the team gave Ford its third Le Mans win in 1969. No other marque has ever won Le Mans two years running; few have won it three times.

A very few "street" GT-40s were built, probably to qualify the car for international production classes. Released for sale starting in early 1966, they were equipped with the milder 289 engine (but retained Weber carbs) and a more civilized interior. About 10 were sold that year for upwards of $15,000 each. A limited run of just seven was offered in 1967 at $18,500 a copy. These cars met all current federal regulations, and all had lefthand drive (most racing GTs were righthand drive).

The best figures currently available, from the Shelby American Automobile Club, show that 123 GT-40s were produced. They represent one of the greatest—probably *the* greatest—Ford competition effort in history. Every GT-40 is now a highly prized collector's item selling for more than even a 427 Cobra. Already recognized as one of Ford's all-time greats, the GT-40 will be long remembered as the epitome of "Total Performance."

Shelby-Mustang

Carroll Shelby's Mustang-based GT-350 appeared only a year after the Mustang itself. It was one of the few truly dual-purpose American production cars; brilliant on the street, and superbly capable on the track. The impetus for it was Ford's desire to give the Mustang a solid performance image. And what better way to do that than by taking the Sports Car Club of America B-production championship from Corvette?

The GT-350 accomplished precisely what it was built for: Jerry Titus won the B-production national championship in 1965. Walt Hane won it again—with the same car— in 1966, and another GT-350 owned the class in 1967. The GT-350 was also successful in drag racing. It was, in a word, a thoroughbred.

There were always two different versions, a street model and a full-house racer. The former existed mainly because of the SCCA rulebook. This required that any model run as a production-class racer had to be built in quantities of at least 100 units annually. The rulebook also took note of a car's passenger capacity, so Shelby made the GT-350 a two-seat sports car by the simple measure of removing the stock Mustang's rear seat and putting the spare tire in the empty space.

Each GT-350 started out as a white Mustang fastback built at Ford's San Jose, California plant and fitted with the 271-bhp high-performance 289 V-8 and Borg-Warner T-10 four-speed transmission. After delivery to Shelby, a High-Riser manifold, big four-barrel carb, and free-flow exhaust headers were added, bringing engine output up to 306 bhp at 6000 rpm. The factory supplied the car with a Ford Galaxie rear axle instead of the stock Falcon unit. This gave a heavier center section and 10 × 3-inch drum brakes, which were fitted with metallic linings. The GT-350's rear axle location was by trailing arms. Koni shocks were used all around. The front suspension was heavily modified with relocated front mounting points and Ford's optional Kelsey-Hayes disc brakes. Shelby also fitted a large front anti-sway bar to provide extra roll stiffness and a heavy steel-tube brace that connected the tops of the front shock absorber towers to eliminate body flex under hard cornering loads. The GT-350 rolled on cast-aluminum, 15-inch-diameter wheels (with 6-inch-wide rims) made by the Shelby factory. They were shod with Goodyear high-performance tires. The stock Mustang steering box was replaced by one with a quicker ratio. The result of all this was near neutral handling, in contrast to the standard Mustang's strong understeer. The GT-350 driver could thus exploit the car's extra power for cornering to the limit.

The GT-350's exterior design was just as carefully thought out. The standard Mustang's prancing pony was plucked from the grille, leaving a simple rectangular opening. The steel hood was replaced by a fiberglass replica with a functional, built-in scoop. The dummy scoops ahead of the rear wheels were opened up to duct cooling air to the rear brakes. On 1966 models the factory fastback's air extractor vents in the rear roof pillars were replaced by plastic windows that

improved outward visibility and gave the Shelby a lighter overall look. Finally, blue racing stripes were applied along the rocker panels. Another pair of much wider stripes split the hood, roof, and rear deck down the center to set off the white paint job. Some later cars were painted blue and had white striping.

The GT-350's interior was mildly altered from that of the production Mustang. The most obvious changes were three-inch-wide seatbelts, a mahogany-rim steering wheel, and full instrumentation. All "street" GTs came with black interiors and stock Mustang seats. For owners who occasionally needed to carry rear passengers, a kit was available with a small bench seat that put the spare tire back in the trunk.

The full-race version was basically the same as the street car, but more highly tuned and specifically set up for the track. The engine in the GT-350R developed 350 bhp. In fact, it was the same unit used in the racing Cobras. The T-10 four-speed was unchanged except for an aluminum case to save weight. The interior was stripped except for a racing bucket seat, rollbar, safety harness, and necessary intruments. A heavy-duty suspension was used along with racing tires. The final touch was a new fiberglass nose that eliminated the front bumper, leaving a rudimentary air dam with a large central slot that acted as an air intake for an oil cooler. Though it looked much like the street car, the racing GT-350 was a very mean machine. Some had four-wheel disc brakes and engines up to 400 hp.

Ford redesigned the Mustang for 1967, making it larger and heavier to suit the big 390 V-8, offered as an option for the first time that year. Shelby American modified this new platform for its '67 GT-350 and a new GT-500 model, the latter packing the enormous 428 V-8. A completely new fiberglass front end and a re-styled rear-end panel with big taillights were fitted to both racing and street versions. Only minor modifications were made to the stock Mustang chassis.

Selling for about $4500, the '67s could not be confused with the original 1965–66 models, which are the blue-chips among Shelby-Mustangs. The 1968 and later cars continued the Shelby name, but were built entirely by Ford and are not as desirable. Still, every Shelby GT was several cuts above the showroom-stock Mustang, and showed just how much depth existed in Ford's basic ponycar package. They were grand touring cars of world-class caliber.

De Tomaso Pantera

Alejandro de Tomaso was an expatriot Argentine who built formula cars and sports racers in the early '60s. He then decided to construct a production sports car to suit his own high standards. His first effort was the mid-engine Vallelunga, equipped with a 1500cc British Ford engine. It was a good car, but not terribly fast.

Its successor, however, was. This was the magnificent Mangusta, designed by Georgetto Guigiaro, one of the world's most talented automobile stylists. His masterful pen produced one of those rare machines

1965 Shelby GT-350

1967 Shelby GT-350

1968 Shelby GT-500KR

1968 Shelby GT-500 Convertible

1968 Shelby GT-500 Fastback

1969 Shelby GT-500 Convertible

that looks perfect from every angle. A low, svelte bullet of a car, it looks better the longer you look at it. It was powered by a Ford 289-cid small-block V-8, mounted behind the driver. Completing the specifications were a ZF five-speed transaxle, a limited-slip differential, and Girling disc brakes at all four wheels. As fast as it was beautiful, the Mangusta had a top speed of 155 mph. Racing car practice even influenced its wheel sizes: the rear ones were larger than the fronts. Complete with air conditioning, the Mangusta sold in the U.S. for only about $11,000.

By 1970, Alejandro de Tomaso, ever the wheeler-dealer, had acquired two respected Italian coach-building firms, Ghia and Vignale. These companies tempted Ford, where styling ideas took the form of lifeless clay models; in Italy, stylists cut their proto-types out of sheet steel with tin snips. Ford bought De Tomaso Automobili, fed Ghia and Vignale into its echelon, and told the Italians to rework the Mangusta.

The result was the De Tomaso Pantera, which was nearly as pretty as the Mangusta and $1000 less expensive. It retained its predecessor's best features such as the mid-engine layout, ZF transaxle, disc brakes, all-independent suspension, and unit body/chassis. But its larger 351-cid Cleveland V-8 produced 310 bhp, which yielded a top speed alleged to be 162 mph.

There were two difficulties, though. In U.S. crash tests, the first Panteras exploded when rammed against the cement barrier. Ford ordered design changes. After a short sales run of about two years, 1974 federal bumper standards spelled the end of Pantera imports. A total of 5269 had been built and sold before this.

1971 De Tomaso Pantera

1973 De Tomaso Pantera

The Pantera was originally marketed in the U.S. through selected Lincoln-Mercury dealers, and carried Ford's normal new-car warranty. But the Pantera was anything but normal: its electrical system frequently gave trouble, and overheating was a problem. These and other trouble spots resulted in Ford partially re-building most of the cars at considerable expense just to keep owners happy. Today, a large national Pantera club with several active regional chapters provides assistance to owners, as well as the usual enthusiast camaraderie.

Although the Pantera was locked out of the American market after 1974, it continued in production for Europe into the 1980s, though at a measly rate of about 25 units annually. Meanwhile, back in the U.S., two of the car's admirers, Steve Hitter and Barry Gale, formed Panteramerica, a company specializing in parts and accessories for the early-'70s models. Through a chance conversation with Alejandro himself, Hitter and Gale were able to reintroduce the Pantera to the U.S. (along with De Tomaso's Longchamps coupe) on a very limited basis starting in 1981.

The revived Pantera is certified for compliance with U.S. safety and emissions standards by an independent firm totally divorced from Ford. The car has been remarkably little changed in the intervening years, as you'd expect with such a low production volume. But there are two noteworthy mechanical differences in the latest versions: the 351-cid power unit now comes from Ford Australia, not Cleveland, and tires are the latest in ultra-grippy, high-performance rubber, Pirelli P7s. *Road & Track* magazine found the "new" Pantera slightly faster than the "old" one (0–60 mph in 6.4 seconds and a 14.9-second quarter-mile versus 7.6 and 15.6 seconds, respectively, for its previous test car), but was dismayed by the much higher price. As the magazine's engineering editor, Dennis Simanaitis, observed: "What with inflation, hand-built limited pro-duction, U.S. legalization and all, the car we looked at cost $59,573, a far cry from the 1973 car's as-tested price of $10,295. In truth, there's probably an argu-ment that one could buy a used Pantera, restore it to pristine condition (or better yet, engineer out some of its shortcomings along the way), pay off all the bills, and still buy a few VW Rabbits with the leftover. On the other hand, we're the first to admit that increased avail-ability of interesting cars—and boring the Pantera definitely isn't—is always good news." Indeed it is.

As for the earlier Panteras, the ones Ford sold in the U.S. were made somewhat differently and in greater numbers compared to the later European models. This means a fair number of used ones are still around at relatively stable prices. Examples in good condition customarily bring from $12,000 to $25,000. That may sound high, but it's peanuts next to what you'd pay for most other Italian exotics.

All in all, this Ford-powered, mid-engine, 150-mph slingshot stands as one of the most exciting "world cars" ever—an Italo-American hybrid of impeccable breeding. And for that reason alone, the Pantera de-serves a special place in Ford's hall of fame.